Garden to Table Cooking

With a Dash of Love

**Transforming your garden and
farmers' market bounty into
easy, delicious, everyday meals**

Linda Engel

Recipes and photos by Linda Engel

GreenThings
🌿Cooking

Published by GreenThings Cooking
Arvada, Colorado

ISBN: 978-0-578-79350-4

Library of Congress Control Number: 2020922149

Light of the Moon, Inc. - Publishing Partners since 2009
Book Design/Production/Consulting
Carbondale, Colorado
www.lightofthemooninc.com

This book is dedicated to
my four beautiful girls:
Grace, Heather, Hannah, and Ashleigh,
and to their beautiful children.
You have all filled my life with
so much love and fun. Thank you.

Acknowledgements

Thank you to my husband, Tom, for being my taste tester, dishwasher, encourager and editor. Thank you Joel, Abby, Collin, Ethan, Sonya, Ashlyn and Ruben Jr. — your commentary on my cooking is an inspiration. Also a big thank you to Anne, Dodie and Mignon for reading my cookbook in the early stages and giving me invaluable feedback. Thank you Diane, Linda and Sue and all those who have encouraged me to complete this project. Thank you to the talented staff at Light of the Moon, Inc. for helping me make this book a reality.

 Table of Contents

*So, whether you eat or drink, or whatever you do,
do all to the glory of God.* (1 Corinthians 10:31)

Introduction	1
About This Book	3
Harvest Staples	5
Soup	21
Salads & Dressings	43
Main Dishes – Beef	63
Main Dishes – Poultry	77
Main Dishes – Vegetarian	97
Side Dishes	119
Desserts & Beverages	131
Index	161
About the Author	165

🌱 Introduction 🌱

*My son, eat honey, for it is good, and the drippings of
the honeycomb are sweet to your taste. Know that wisdom is
such to your soul; if you find it, there will be a future,
and your hope will not be cut off.* (Proverbs 24:13-14)

Gardening. Cooking. Loving. What do these have in common? They are nurturing. Nurturing for the body, mind and soul. The anticipation of things to come when taking a walk in a newly planted garden to inspect for any new sprouts brings such joy. It's so hard at that time to believe

the barren ground will bear an oasis of bounty in just a few months. There is such pleasure in sitting down to a meal grown and prepared by one's own hands. And there is so much joy in showing others how much you love them by presenting a beautifully crafted meal.

When I was younger, I never liked to cook. I never even liked food that much. If there was a pill that I could have taken to replace meals,

I would have taken it. And then in mid-life I started gardening. And then I loved to cook. And then I loved to eat. It was that simple.

And then I had a new way of showing others how I love them — by preparing delicious, healthy food for them. I'd lay awake at night and dream and imagine what new

dish I could make and how I would present it, or how I would put up the abundance of produce ripening on the plants outside.

My new passion became scouring cooking magazines, cookbooks and family recipes. I collected vintage cookbooks and pioneer cookbooks from yard sales and thrift stores. Books about unusual foods. Books about U.S. Presidents' favorite recipes. Books about foraging for food.

INTRODUCTION

Books about the roots of food. Recipes are for me about ideas and imagining what can be.

This book shares the recipes I have created from those ideas and that I use season after season to put up the food we grow so that we can enjoy it all winter long. It's an all-consuming job in the fall, but then the winter and spring cooking are made much easier and more enjoyable. Company coming? No problem — pull a sauce out of the freezer, cook up some chicken, a few vegetables and voila!

This book also shares how I love others through these recipes. Whenever my grandchildren say, "Grandma this is yummy, what did you put in it?" I respond, "There's a very special ingredient in there." And they say, "We know, Grandma, it's love." Can you imagine how the world would change if every child knew this love?

So much is lost in today's world of fast food and isolation, especially for our youth and elderly. But it doesn't have to be lost. Make someone a special meal with that special ingredient — LOVE — and you will see a life light up.

This book is a self-portrait because I share how I express my love, from the seed that I plant through the dish that I make from its bounty. I hope it will inspire you to love others through your own cooking. If you are reading this book, I imagine you already have so much to give.

Need I say the recipes in this book were born in my garden?

What's in a spoon? Love. Years of it. This photo is of the spoon my mother used since early in her 53 years of marriage to my father. She used this spoon to mix countless pots of soup, stews, sauces and much more for her family and friends. Of all the family heirlooms my parents left me, this is the one thing I treasure the most. Why? Because it is full of memories and love.

🌱 About this Book 🌱

Jesus said to them, "I am the bread of life; whoever comes to me
shall not hunger, and whoever believes in me shall never thirst."
(John 6:35)

Simple. My recipes are simple to make. I'm not a complicated cook and I get overwhelmed if there are too many ingredients and too many steps. I use sea salt and herbs abundantly and love to taste the symphony of flavors from the fresh, organic ingredients.

Organic. I am an organic gardener. And I'm not a complicated gardener. I believe in a good, organic soil, some seeds or seedlings, water, sunshine and a grateful heart. Once things are planted, you will often find me in the garden thanking God for whatever harvest He will provide. And I talk to my plants. Sometimes in English and sometimes in Italian, but always with a soft, kind voice. I am sure I've heard them speak back to me at times.

The meat, chicken and eggs I use are from organic, grass-fed, free-range roving animals. I believe this is healthier and kinder. The tofu I use is organic, non-GMO. I also believe this is healthier and better for our farmlands.

Ohne late summer, our grandson Ruben Jr. (at six years old) was staying with us for a couple of days. It's the time of year when garden vegetables fill all available counter space while they wait to be used. He was playing around in the kitchen and dining room and all of a sudden got very quiet and looked at me. After a moment he said, "Grandma Linda, your house is full of God and vegetables. I think I might be in heaven." I'm sure I could see God smiling. I was, too. From ear to ear. ♥

Gluten Free. Because I eat a gluten-free diet, my recipes are gluten-free. But the recipes allow for your choice of grain type.

Abundance. My excuse for planting too much is that I will be able to share with my neighbors and friends. What a joy.

Curiosity. Some of the recipes might sound odd, but give them a try; you will find them alive with fresh flavor and nutrition. Many are also family and company pleasers as well.

Rhythm. Spring is busy with planting and anticipating. Summer is busy with tending. Fall is busy with harvesting and making all kinds of concoctions for later consumption. Winter is busy with resting and enjoying the fruits of the harvest. When February comes, it is time to start dreaming of what to grow in the spring. And on the cycle goes. A beautiful rhythm of love.

A note on cooking times: the cooking times in this book reflect cooking at a mile-high altitude (5,280 feet). If you live at a lower elevation, you will need to slightly decrease the cooking time. If you live at a higher elevation, you will need to slightly increase the cooking time.

 Harvest Staples

*And you shall eat and be full and you
shall bless the Lord your God for the good land
he has given you.* (Deuteronomy 8:10)

I soon realized that if I was going to garden, I was going to have to figure out what to do with everything I was growing. The recipes in this chapter are where I started. Staples that I could put up and use throughout the winter, staples to enjoy some of that summer "yum" and sunshine when it's cold outside. The recipes flourished from this chapter forward.

There comes a time each season when I hear the vegetables in the garden speaking to me with urgency. "It's time … If you don't start doing something with us, we'll go bad." Then each day is planned around what will be harvested and put up and how it will be put up. I've never taken the time to figure out canning, so for me it's all about how to freeze the bounty — as the vegetable itself, made into a sauce, roasted or as part of something else. It's a delight to plan my winter, spring and early summer cooking around what is in the freezer.

Most of the recipes in this chapter are used throughout the book as ingredients for other recipes.

BBQ Sauce	6
Cayenne Pepper	7
Chimichurri Sauce	8
Enchilada Sauce	9
Green Beans	10
Pesto	11
Pickled Jalapeños	12
Poblano Peppers, Roasted	13
Pumpkin	14
Spaghetti Squash	15
Stevia	16
Tomatillo Sauce	18
Tomato Paste	19
Tomato Sauce	20

BBQ Sauce

I love a good BBQ sauce. It took me two seasons of trials to come up with one that was everything I wanted it to be: smooth, a bit tangy, spicy to taste but not to linger, and with layers of flavors.

I use this sauce to make the BBQ Beef and BBQ Chicken Sandwiches (see Main Dishes). It also freezes well. I freeze it in two-cup containers, which makes it easy to pull out and make a quick dinner of BBQ sandwiches along with some roasted vegetables.

Servings: about 6 cups

Ingredients
    3 pounds ripe tomatoes, quartered
    1 medium onion, chopped
    3 garlic cloves, minced
    1 tablespoon black peppercorns
    2 teaspoons celery seeds
    1 teaspoon paprika
    2 whole cloves
    ¼ teaspoon dry mustard
    ¼ teaspoon cayenne pepper
    ⅓ cup brown sugar or molasses
    ¼ cup apple cider vinegar
    1 teaspoon sea salt

Directions
1. In a large pot, combine tomatoes, onion, garlic and all spices and bring to simmer.
2. Cook until soft and juicy, about 30 minutes. Let cool.
3. Put tomato mixture in blender and blend at highest speed until smooth.
4. Run mixture through food mill using finest screen. This step is not necessary if you are using a high powered blender.

5. Return to pot and add sweetener, vinegar and salt.
6. Cook until blended and thick, about 20 minutes.
7. Adjust seasonings and sweetener to taste.

Cayenne Pepper

I always shied away from cayenne pepper because of how hot everyone said it was. Then one year I accidently bought a four-pack of cayenne peppers and had no choice but to plant them. Thus a love affair began.

I grow a new crop every year. Of all the things I grow, believe it or not, cayenne is my favorite. There is no comparison between homegrown and store-bought cayenne.

Growing and Drying Notes

1. When growing cayenne peppers, let them turn red on the bush before picking, if possible. If the season runs out on you, you can pick them green and they will turn red as they dry.
2. Once picked, string the peppers through the stems using a needle and thread.
3. Hang the strings of peppers over a curtain rod in a sunny window. Be sure it's in an area with ventilation.
4. When the peppers are completely dry, take them down and remove from the string.
5. Store in a glass container with a lid.

Using the Cayenne Peppers

Use the peppers by popping off the stem end and grinding the dried pepper (seeds included) with a mortar and pestle or in a spice grinder. Add to just about any dish to add an amazing flavor. You can find instructions online for grinding the peppers into a powder. See Important Note below.

Important Note

Use the same cautions when handling cayenne peppers as you would when handling any other hot pepper. Wear gloves because if you use your bare hands, even when you wash them afterwards, the oil will stay on your skin for a while. Do not touch your eyes, nose, mouth or anyone else.

DO NOT ATTEMPT TO MAKE FINELY GROUND CAYENNE PEPPER WITHOUT USING EYE PROTECTION, FACE MASK AND GLOVES.

Chimichurri Sauce

I am addicted to this sauce. Hardly a day goes by when I don't put it on something. It's delicious on eggs, chicken, fish or beef, potatoes, artichokes and just about anything else you want to put it on. I use it on my sandwiches as a replacement for mayonnaise. I make dozens of four-ounce jars of this during the growing season and freeze it for off-season use.

Flat-leaf parsley and oregano are both easy to grow.

Servings: about 2 cups

Ingredients

4 cups fresh flat-leaf parsley, packed
1 cup fresh oregano leaves, pulled off stems
1 cup olive oil
½ cup red wine vinegar
3 garlic cloves, peeled and minced
1 teaspoon cayenne pepper flakes
1 teaspoon sea salt

Directions

1. Place all items in a food processor and process a few pulses at a time until roughly ground; do not make the sauce smooth, it is meant to have bits of herbs in it.
2. Store in the refrigerator or freeze for future use.

Notes

- Dry the herbs well after washing them. I use a salad spinner and that works great.
- Mince the garlic before adding because you will not process the sauce enough for the food processor to do so.
- This sauce is meant to be a bit oily.

Enchilada Sauce

I used to get stressed out when it came time to make a red enchilada sauce because all the recipes I came across seemed complicated (too many steps for me). So I decided to come up with one that was simple and still tasty.

I grow Anaheim peppers to make this sauce and allow them to turn red on the bush, or the counter, if I must pick them due to a frost warning. I dry them by stringing them on thread and hanging in a window. When they are completely dry, I store them in a glass jar until I am ready to use them.

This sauce mixes well with ground beef to make taco meat, can be used to make enchiladas, put on eggs, etc. — it is very versatile. It freezes well; I freeze it in one-cup glass containers.

Servings: 5 to 6 cups

Ingredients
    4 cups water, vegetable, chicken or beef stock
    12–15 dried Anaheim peppers (or other chili pepper)
    2 tablespoons olive oil
    1 small onion, chopped
    3 cloves of garlic, minced
    1 teaspoon cumin
    2 paste tomatoes, chopped
    1 tablespoon oregano
    2 tablespoons red wine vinegar
    1 tablespoon sea salt

Directions
1. Boil water or stock; remove from heat and set aside.
2. Prepare the peppers: (be sure to wear gloves) remove stem and seeds and tear/cut chilies into pieces.
3. In a large cast iron skillet or saucepan, heat oil over medium heat. Add peppers, onions and garlic. Sauté until fragrant and onion is soft, about 5 minutes.
4. Add cumin and tomatoes and mix well.
5. Slowly add hot liquid. Mix, bring to a boil, then cover and simmer until peppers are hydrated and soft, about 30 minutes.
6. Add oregano, vinegar and sea salt.
7. Blend until smooth.

Green Beans

Freezing green beans is a very easy process, and it is rewarding to pull the green beans out of the freezer and add them to other dishes in the off-season. I add them to Beef Stew and Mung Dal and Basmati Rice (see Main Dishes) and use them to make Green Bean and Vegetable Soup (see Soup). I even save the blanching water (from the pot, not the sink) and use it as the liquid for my smoothies or as a vegetable stock to add to soups and stews.

These instructions are for blanching and freezing one pound of green beans at a time.

Directions
1. Wash beans and remove stem ends.
2. Cut into bite-size pieces, about 1 inch.
3. Fill a saucepan or skillet with 3–4 inches of water and bring to a rolling boil.
4. Fill your sink with 3–4 inches of water and add several cups of ice.

5. Add the cut green beans to the boiling water and blanch for 3 minutes.
6. Remove the green beans from the boiling water and add immediately to the ice water.
7. Leave them in the ice water until they are completely cooled.
8. Drain them from the ice water and shake off extra water.
9. Line a rimmed cookie sheet or casserole dish with parchment paper.
10. Lay the green beans in a single layer on the parchment paper and place the dish in the freezer until the beans are frozen.
11. Remove the beans from the parchment paper and place in a suitable freezer container.
12. Label with contents and date; place in freezer.

Pesto

In Italy, I've heard pesto called liquid gold. The flavor is amazing and delights the palate. I use it on pasta (see Pasta with Pesto & Chicken in Main Dishes), on sandwiches in place of mayonnaise (see Turkey Sandwiches — 4 Ways in Main Dishes), to make Chicken Pesto Salad (see Salads & Dressings), Chicken Pesto Pizza, Pizza with Tofu (see Main Dishes), and so much more. The recipe doubles easily.

I grow Mammoth Basil, as shown in the photo. It produces leaves large enough to make small wraps.

Servings: 1½ cups

Ingredients

- 3 cups packed basil
- ½ cup olive oil
- ¼ cup pine nuts
- ¼ cup parmesan cheese
- 2 cloves garlic, peeled
- ½ teaspoon sea salt

Directions
Place all ingredients in blender and blend until smooth.

Variations
- Use half basil and half parsley.
- Use 1 cup each basil, parsley, sage.
- Replace the pine nuts with walnuts or pumpkin seeds.
- Leave out the garlic and/or parmesan if you are sensitive to either.

Notes
- Freeze in 4-ounce jars for use long after the garden is over.
- Freeze in an ice cube tray and then remove the cubes from the tray and keep frozen in a plastic bag or glass freezer container. One cube is perfect for several sandwiches, a serving of pasta, or a batch of Chicken Pesto Salad (see Salads & Dressings).

Pickled Jalapeños

One season I had a bumper crop of jalapeños and was wondering how I could preserve them and enjoy them all winter. I decided to give pickled jalapeños a try, and it was good enough to make again. This recipe is easy, doesn't require canning and will last through the winter in the refrigerator (if they last that long!).

Servings: two 8-ounce jars

Ingredients
- 1 cup filtered water
- 1 cup distilled white vinegar
- 1 tablespoon sugar
- 1 tablespoon sea salt
- 2 garlic cloves, peeled and smashed
- ¼ teaspoon dried oregano (optional)
- ¼ teaspoon dried cilantro (optional)
- 15–20 jalapeños, sliced and stem discarded

Directions
1. In a saucepan combine water, vinegar, sugar, salt, garlic and herbs, if using.
2. Bring to a boil, stir to dissolve sugar and salt.
3. Turn off heat and add jalapeños. Stir so they are all submerged and let sit for 15 minutes.
4. Divide jalapeños between two 8-ounce glass jars, cover with pickling juices.
5. Put lids on jars and refrigerate.

Note
Jalapeños also freeze well — wash, dry and place them in a suitable freezer container. To use, remove just a few minutes before using and slice or chop while still slightly frozen.

Poblano Peppers, Roasted

Roasted poblano peppers impart an intensely delicious flavor to any dish. When I grow them, I've found that they can be very hot or very mild. I sample them before using them so I know how much, or how little, to use in my dish.

Although roasted poblano peppers get most of the attention, I also use them fresh and chopped like other peppers and enjoy them just as much. I add these delicious peppers to salads, frittatas, soups, stews and — when I have an abundance of them — to just about anything that I prepare.

Poblano peppers freeze well, whether roasted or fresh, and it's nice to have a stash in the freezer to add to dishes.

Ingredients
   Poblano peppers

Directions
   1. Heat oven to 400°F.
   2. Wash and dry peppers.
   3. On a cookie sheet, place the peppers with an inch or so between them.
   4. Place the sheet in the oven and roast until top skins are blistered and charred. Then turn the peppers. Continue this until all sides of the peppers are blistered.
   5. When all sides of peppers are blistered, remove from oven and place the peppers in a bowl and cover bowl with a plate.
   6. When peppers have cooled, remove charred skins, stems and seeds.

Options
   There are several ways to prepare peppers for freezing. I prepare them according to the recipe in which I anticipate using them:
   1. Chopped poblano: remove charred skins, stems and seeds. Chop and freeze in freezer bags or glass containers.
   2. Whole poblano: Freeze as is after roasting. When you go to use them, the charred skin removes easily after a few minutes of defrosting.
   3. For stuffing: remove charred skins and seeds, leaving stem in.

Pumpkin

Growing, roasting, processing and cooking with homegrown pumpkin is a special treat. There's no comparison between homegrown and store-bought pumpkin. Homegrown is lighter, sweeter and bursting with flavor. If you are going to grow them, be sure to select pie pumpkin seeds or starts; these are smaller and sweeter. Pumpkin freezes well and this is a great way to ensure there is always some on hand.

Directions to Roast and Process a Homegrown Pie Pumpkin

1. Place oven rack on the lowest shelf.
2. Heat oven to 400°F.
3. Remove the stem from the pumpkin.
4. Wash the pumpkin well, especially the blossom and stem ends. Dry it with a towel.
5. Using a small, sharp utensil (I use a metal skewer) poke 4 to 5 small holes in the bottom of the pumpkin.
6. Place a rack over a baking pan and place the pumpkin on the rack. This allows the liquid to drain out of the pumpkin through the holes and be captured in the pan.

7. Roast for 60 to 90 minutes. It's done when a knife slips into the flesh like butter.
8. Remove the pumpkin from the oven and let it cool.
9. Slice pumpkin in half. Be careful that any escaping steam does not burn you.

10. Remove the seeds and peel the pumpkin. If the skin sticks, scoop out the pumpkin from the skin.
11. Place pumpkin in a food processor and purée until smooth.
12. Freeze what you will not be using in the next day or two. I freeze the pumpkin in glass containers in the serving size called for in my favorite recipes.

Spaghetti Squash

Spaghetti squash is delicious, nutritious, versatile and stores for a long time in a cool environment. I'm often finishing up the crop from the previous year when it's time to plant the new year's crop. Sauté the cooked squash with butter, chives and salt as a side dish. Use it as a substitute for pasta, or use it in a myriad of other recipes (see Main Dishes and Side Dishes). The cooked squash also freezes well.

Directions to Cook a Spaghetti Squash
1. Heat oven to 375°F.
2. Remove the stem and wash the squash with soap and water then dry. If the stem is too hard to break off cut it off after you cut the squash in half.
3. Cut the squash in half from the stem to the blossom end and remove the seeds.
4. In a glass baking dish, place the squash open end down. If it's a large squash, you might need to use two dishes.
5. Pour in enough water to just cover the lip of the squash.
6. Bake for 40 minutes, or until squash strings are tender and easily removed from the shell with a fork.

7. Use caution when removing the dish from the oven so that you don't spill or burn yourself with the hot water. I remove the squash using tongs or forks and place them on a rack, plate or the counter and let them cool prior to removing the strings.

8. Remove the strings using a fork and/or spoon.
9. Your squash is now ready to be eaten.

Stevia

Stevia is easy and fun to grow. I love to watch the expression on people's faces when I offer them a leaf and invite them to taste it and see if they can tell me what it is. No one expects a green leaf to taste like a piece of candy!

You can use the leaves fresh from the plant in your tea or coffee to sweeten it or dry and grind the leaves to use as a powder. Yes, it's green, but it tastes so much better than the white processed stevia available in the stores. It is VERY sweet, and a little goes a long way.

In late fall, after I've harvested the stevia and the plant is just a stalk, I overwinter it in our garage. I water it occasionally and on warm, sunny days, which we have in Colorado in the winter, I bring it out in the sun. When spring comes, I move the pot outside and it grows back. It's really remarkable.

I have read several different ways to dry stevia. Here is how I dry and process mine. I live in a dry climate, so I can dry herbs in a couple days in hot, sunny weather. If you live in a humid climate, please do some reading on how to dry herbs properly in your area. You want them to be completely dry before you store them to prevent mold from growing.

Stevia continued

Directions

1. Harvest the stevia at the end of the growing season as the weather begins to cool and in the morning before the day heats up.
2. Cut the branches off the trunk.
3. Pull the leaves off the branches.
4. Rinse the leaves and dry them; a salad spinner works well for this.
5. Line a baking pan with parchment paper and place a cooling rack on top of it.
6. Lay the stevia leaves on the rack in a single layer.
7. Place the pan in a warm spot that has good air circulation. I place them on the chair on my patio and push the chair under the patio table. The sun shines through the slots, enough to speed the drying but not enough to burn the leaves.
8. Move the leaves around every couple of hours. I bring the leaves inside in late afternoon and place them in a dry spot with good air circulation to finish drying.
9. When the leaves are completely dry, they will crumble easily between your fingers.
10. Use either a blender or an herb grinder to powder the leaves.

Tomatillo Sauce

One taste of this and you'll be hooked. This sauce is very versatile; it can be used on chicken, enchiladas, fajitas, burritos, rice or anything you'd like. It freezes very well, and in the dead of winter taking some out and smothering a piece of chicken is like inviting your summer garden back for a visit.

Some people may be a bit hesitant because it's green, but just tell them to close their eyes and take a taste and the hesitancy will dissipate immediately.

Servings: 6 to 8 cups

Ingredients
      3 tablespoons olive oil
      8 cups of quartered tomatillos (remove husks and wash first)
      1 onion, chopped
      4 Anaheim peppers, stem and seeds removed and chopped
      2 poblano peppers, stem and seeds removed and chopped
      4 cloves of garlic, chopped
      2 cups chicken stock (add more or less for desired consistency)
      1 teaspoon sea salt

Directions
   1. In a large saucepan over medium, heat the olive oil.
   2. Add tomatillos, onion and peppers; sauté for a couple of minutes until fragrant.
   3. Add garlic and chicken stock and cook until tomatillos are broken down and very soft, about 30 to 40 minutes.
   4. Add sea salt.
   5. Cool and blend until smooth.

Tomato Paste

You may be wondering why in the world one would want to go through the trouble of making homemade tomato paste. I tried it once because I had so many tomatoes from the garden that I needed to make something that would use a bunch of them up. I've never looked back AND haven't purchased store-bought paste since. Homemade tomato paste is not quite as thick or as red as store bought, but the flavor is so amazing.

My favorite tomatoes to grow for paste are San Marzano and Polish Linguisa. They are indeterminate plants and produce large plum tomatoes that are dark red, firm and delicious. However, any plum tomato will taste great.

Servings: 2 to 3 cups

Ingredients
   5 pounds of ripe tomatoes, coarsely chopped
   ½ cup olive oil
   1 teaspoon sea salt

Directions
   1. Heat oven to 300°F.
   2. To a large pot add olive oil, tomatoes and salt.
   3. Bring to a boil and cook until just soft, about 5 minutes.
   4. Run tomatoes through a food mill to remove skins and seeds.
   5. Pour tomato pulp into a large rimmed baking sheet.
   6. Bake for 3 hours, stirring every 30 minutes. Be sure to stir in the caramelized sauce that forms around the edges.
   7. Reduce oven temperature to 250°F and continue cooking and stirring every 30 minutes to desired thickness.
   8. Freeze in ice cube trays; each cube is 2 tablespoons. When frozen, remove from the ice cube tray and place in a suitable freezer container.

Tomato Sauce

Imagine a warm, late summer evening, sitting outside on your patio and taking the first bite of pasta with a tomato sauce from tomatoes just picked and cooked. I'm not sure there is a better taste in the world. I serve this over all types of pasta with grilled chicken on the side or cubed and mixed in with the pasta. Add Zucchini Parmesan Rounds (see Side Dishes) on the side and it's a perfect match.

My favorite plum tomatoes to grow are San Marzano and Polish Linguisa.

Servings: 3 to 4 cups

Ingredients

    2 tablespoons olive oil
    ½ medium onion, diced
    2 cloves garlic, minced
    2 pounds plum tomatoes, chopped
    ¼ cup chopped fresh basil (or 1 tablespoon dried basil)
    ¼ cup chopped fresh oregano (or 1 tablespoon dried basil)
    ½ teaspoon sea salt
    ¼ teaspoon cayenne pepper flakes

Directions

1. In a large pot over medium, heat the olive oil.
2. Add onion and sauté until soft, about 5 minutes.
3. Add garlic, sauté for another minute.
4. Add remaining ingredients and cook until tomatoes are completely broken down, about 30 minutes.

Note

This sauce will be very thick and chunky (not to mention delicious). If you prefer it to be smoother, run it through a food mill or blend it in a high-speed blender.

 Soup

...and there you shall eat before the Lord your God, and you shall rejoice, you and your households, in all that you undertake, in which the Lord your God has blessed you. (Deuteronomy 12:7)

Soup. What a wonderful, nutritious comfort food. Who doesn't love a nice steaming hot bowl of soup on a cool fall day or cold winter evening? Soups are a great one-pot meal that can be packed with a lot of nutrition. I make large batches and freeze the extra for a quick meal or for those times when the grandchildren are over in the middle of winter and say, "Grandma, can you make zucchini soup?" No worries; I pull it out of the freezer and everyone's happy and full before long.

Black Bean Soup	22
Buckwheat Noodle Soup	23
Butternut Squash Soup	24
Cauliflower Soup	25
Chicken Soup	26
Chicken Stock	27
Chicken Tomatillo Soup	28
Green Bean Vegetable Soup	29
Miso Soup	30
Potato Soup	31
Pumpkin Soup	32
Ramen Soup	33
Sausage Vegetable Noodle Soup	34
Southwest Chicken Soup	35
Steamed Vegetable Soup	36
Tomato Soup	37
Vegetable Broth	38
Vegetable Soup	39
White Bean & Vegetable Soup	40
Zucchini Soup	41

Black Bean Soup

While this recipe does not use a lot of garden vegetables, it still makes a delicious meal. Canned beans work great and are very convenient, but buy the dried beans and soak and cook them just once and you'll never turn back. The corn bread pictured is a variation of the Corn Muffin recipe in Side Dishes.

Servings: 5 to 6

Ingredients
    3 tablespoons olive oil
    1 onion, chopped
    2 carrots, chopped
    4 cups black beans, cooked
    4 cups liquid*
    2 cloves garlic, minced
    2 teaspoons oregano
    1 teaspoon cumin
    1 teaspoon sea salt
    ¼ teaspoon cayenne pepper flakes

*If you soak and cook your own black beans, you can use the liquid in which the beans cook and add chicken stock, vegetable stock or water to equal the 4 cups. If you use canned black beans, drain and rinse them and then use 4 cups of liquid of choice.

Directions
    1. In a large soup pot over medium, heat olive oil.
    2. Add onion and cook until the onions are translucent, about 5 minutes.
    3. Add carrots. Cook for another minute or two.
    4. Add remaining ingredients.
    5. Bring to a boil, then reduce to a simmer and cover.
    6. Cook for 15 to 20 minutes until flavors are well blended.
    7. Purée with a hand blender to desired consistency. I prefer it still a little chunky.

Variation
    • Add 2 diced purple potatoes (or small potatoes of choice) in Step 3.
    • Add 1 cup of cooked, shredded chicken in Step 4.
    • Then add remaining ingredients and cook long enough for the potatoes to be soft.
    • Barely blend, leaving the soup very chunky.

Buckwheat Noodle Soup

This is an easy-to-make, satisfying meal. The sky is the limit as to the vegetables and spices you can use. Here is my favorite version.

Servings: 2

Ingredients
   1 package buckwheat noodles
   3 cups chicken or vegetable stock
   2 baby bok choy, chopped
   2 carrots, chopped
   1 small head (and some stem) broccoli, chopped
   ¼ teaspoon cayenne pepper flakes
   Sea salt to taste

Directions
   1. Cook noodles according to package instructions, drain, rinse and set aside.
   2. In a medium pot, combine remaining ingredients and cook until vegetables are just tender, about 10 minutes.
   3. Run a knife through the noodles to cut into bite-size pieces and place desired amount in each soup bowl.
   4. Cover noodles with desired amount of soup.

Butternut Squash Soup

Butternut squash is a regular in my summer garden. It is easy to grow and it's fun to count how many develop on the vines and to watch them grow all summer. This soup is a delicious way to enjoy the squash.

Servings: 6 to 8

Ingredients

3 tablespoons olive oil
1 leek, sliced in rounds
1 butternut squash, peeled, seeded and chopped
1 potato, chopped
2 carrots, chopped
2 celery stalks, chopped
2 tablespoons minced fresh rosemary (or 1 tablespoon dried)
1 tablespoon fresh thyme (or ½ tablespoon dried)
Sea salt to taste
4 cups chicken stock
Pumpkin seeds (optional)

Directions

1. In a soup pot over medium, heat the olive oil.
2. Add all vegetables and spices and cook until fragrant, about 7 to 8 minutes.
3. Add stock and simmer, covered, until all vegetables are soft, about 30 minutes.
4. Blend until smooth.
5. Top with pumpkin seeds if desired.

Cauliflower Soup

This soup is easy to make and so good. Add cooked rice or quinoa and some cooked chicken to the soup to make it a full meal.

Servings: 4 to 6

Ingredients
   2 tablespoons olive oil
   1 medium head of cauliflower, chopped
   1 leek, chopped
   2 carrots, chopped
   2 celery stalks, chopped
   4 cups chicken stock
   Sea salt to taste
   Chives
   Parmesan cheese, grated

Directions
   1. In a large soup pot over medium, heat olive oil.
   2. Add all vegetables and sauté until fragrant, 5 to 10 minutes.
   3. Add chicken stock and cook until vegetables are tender.
   4. Blend to desired consistency.
   5. Add sea salt.
   6. Top with chives and grated parmesan cheese to serve.

Chicken Soup

With chicken stock in the freezer, this is an easy and nutritious meal to pull together. Who doesn't feel rejuvenated and comforted after a hot bowl of chicken noodle or chicken rice soup?

Servings: 4 to 6

Ingredients
4 cups chicken stock
½ onion, chopped
3 carrots, chopped
3 celery stalks, chopped
½ cup sliced okra (optional)
1 cup chopped cooked chicken
2 cups cooked brown or white rice, wild rice, or noodles
Sea salt and pepper to taste

Directions
1. In a large soup pot, combine all ingredients, except rice or noodles, and bring to a simmer.
2. Cover and cook until vegetables are desired tenderness, about 20 minutes.
3. Add cooked rice or noodles and cook until heated.

Note
If you are making enough soup so there will be leftovers and are using noodles, put the noodles in the bowls and pour the hot soup over them rather than adding them to the soup pot. If you add the noodles to the pot, the noodles will absorb the liquid and the texture will change as it sits in the refrigerator.

Chicken Stock

Chicken stock can be enjoyed on its own as well as used in so many dishes. It is a staple in my cooking and always on hand in the freezer. If I am feeling run down or don't feel like eating much but want some nutrition, I heat up a cup or two of this, add some sea salt and enjoy the warmth and nutrition. I freeze this in one and two-cup glass freezer containers — it makes it easy to grab the amount needed.

How much this makes will depend on how long you let the stock cook; the longer it cooks, the more reduced and concentrated it will be.

My mother lived with us in her later years and one day she was not feeling well. I served her up a bowl of fresh chicken stock from the stove, and with her first spoonful she said, "Ah, just how my mother used to make it." She smiled through the entire bowl and her health and vitality were quickly restored. Love in a bowl full of precious memories.

Servings: about 4 quarts

Ingredients
  6 quarts of water
  1 whole chicken, cleaned and cut up
  3 carrots, chopped
  4 celery stalks (tops included), chopped
  1 onion, quartered
  1 handful fresh parsley, leaves and stems

Directions
  1. To a large stock pot add 6 quarts of water.
  2. Wash and cut up chicken, put in stock pot, include skin.
  3. Add carrots, celery and onion.
  4. Bring to a boil.
  5. Skim foam off.
  6. Reduce heat to a simmer and cover.
  7. After about 45 minutes pull out bones and cut off meat then return the bones to the pot, reserving the meat for other uses.
  8. Cover and simmer on very low heat, so water is just moving, for 6 to 24 hours.
  9. Add the parsley and simmer for 15 minutes.
  10. Turn off heat and cool.
  11. Strain off the stock, discarding remaining bones and vegetables.

Chicken Tomatillo Soup

This is a hearty and delicious soup. Serve with corn muffins (see Side Dishes), chips or quesadillas and you have a nice meal. It freezes well too.

Servings: 4 to 6

Ingredients

3 pounds tomatillos, outer husks removed, washed and quartered
4 Anaheim peppers (you can also use poblano peppers)
1 onion, chopped
2 medium russet potatoes, chopped
1 medium zucchini, chopped
4 cups chicken stock
1 cup chopped cooked chicken
1 cup corn, fresh or frozen
Sea salt and pepper to taste

Directions

1. In a large soup pot, combine tomatillos, peppers, onion, potatoes, zucchini and stock.
2. Bring to a boil, cover and simmer until vegetables are tender, about 20 minutes.
3. Add chicken.
4. Blend to desired consistency (an immersion blender works great).
5. Add corn and salt.
6. Reheat and serve.

One night when our grandchildren Joel and Abby were over, we served this soup for dinner along with quesadillas. Our grandson does not like cheese so we put turkey in his. After a couple of bites, he looked at me and said, "Mmm, this is good, you should put this in your cookbook, Grandma." He munched away, dipping his quesadilla in his soup. "Grandma, explain it just like this: you take the quesadilla and dip it in the soup, then it changes the flavor to perfect. Mmmm."

Green Bean Vegetable Soup

Don't let this simple sounding recipe fool you; it is surprisingly delicious and comforting, and it freezes well. When I put up green beans from the garden (see Harvest Staples), I freeze them in one-pound portions so I can easily make more of this soup when my freezer stock runs out.

Servings: 5 to 6

Ingredients
4 cups chicken stock
1 pound of green beans, ends cut off and chopped
4 cups of chopped zucchini
2 cups chopped swiss chard
2 cups flat-leaf parsley, chopped
2 celery stalks, chopped
Sea salt to taste

Directions
1. In a large soup pot, combine all ingredients, bring to a boil, turn heat down and simmer until vegetables are tender, about 30 minutes.
2. Add sea salt.
3. Blend with immersion blender.

Miso Soup

This is a simple, satisfying soup that works well for breakfast, lunch or dinner. You can easily change up the vegetables based on what you have on hand. My favorite is bok choy, so that is what I've used here. Bok choy is easy to grow.

Servings: 2 to 3

Ingredients
   4 cups water, vegetable or chicken stock
   2 baby bok choy, chopped
   1 cup chopped spinach
   5 ounces organic firm tofu, chopped
   1-inch piece ginger root, grated
   ¼ cup miso
   4 green onions, diced

Directions
   1. In a large soup pot, combine all ingredients except miso and green onions.
   2. Simmer until vegetables are slightly softened, about 10 minutes.
   3. Turn off heat.
   4. Mix miso in a couple tablespoons of water to dissolve (if you add to the water without doing this step you will get clumps).
   5. Mix miso mixture into soup.
   6. Serve and sprinkle with green onions.

Potato Soup

This simple soup is packed with flavor. Don't skimp on the herbs, they are what will make your taste buds sing.

Servings: 4 to 6

Ingredients

2 tablespoons olive oil
2 leeks, coarsely chopped
5 medium russet potatoes, washed and chopped (peeling optional)
1 quart chicken stock
2 tablespoons minced fresh parsley
1 tablespoon minced fresh rosemary
Sea salt and black pepper to taste
Chives (optional)

One day, my granddaughter Abby (at 10 years old) and I went out for a "girls" morning. We returned home to this delicious pot of soup made by my husband and Abby's 11-year-old brother, Joel. When I asked my grandson what it was that made it so delicious, guess what he said?
"Love."

Directions

1. In a large soup pot over medium, heat olive oil.
2. Add the leeks and sauté until aromatic (but not browned).
3. Add potatoes, chicken stock and herbs.
4. Cook until potatoes are tender.
5. Blend until almost smooth.
6. Return to pot, add salt and pepper and reheat.
7. Stir to keep soup from sticking on the bottom.
8. Serve with fresh chives.

Pumpkin Soup

It took me years to get up the gump-tion to eat pumpkin soup. But, one year a bumper crop of pie pumpkins forced the issue. You'll find this pumpkin soup more savory than it is sweet; in fact, it's not sweet at all. Served alongside some Socca (you can find the recipe online — it's a wonderful pancake-type bread made from chickpea flour), it makes a light and satisfying meal.

Servings: 4 to 6

Ingredients
    1 tablespoon olive oil
    1 leek, sliced
    3 celery stalks, chopped
    3 cups pumpkin purée (see Harvest Staples)
    4 cups chicken stock (or vegetable stock)
    2 tablespoons minced fresh rosemary
    Sea salt to taste
    Pumpkin seeds

Directions
    1. In a large soup pot over medium, heat olive oil.
    2. Add leeks and celery, sauté until soft, about 10 minutes.
    3. Add pumpkin, chicken stock and rosemary.
    4. Cook for 15 to 20 minutes until flavors are melded.
    5. Using a hand-held blender, blend to almost smooth, leaving some small chunks for texture.
    6. Add sea salt.
    7. Sprinkle with pumpkin seeds and serve.

Note
    This soup tastes best when made slightly thick but not too thick. Add more stock or a bit of water if necessary.

Ramen Soup

There's so much more to ramen soup than the 25-cent packages we see at the supermarket. Ramen noodles, broth, meat and vegetables make a quick, delicious and satisfying meal. You can also find delicious, gluten-free ramen noodles in the health food stores.

Servings: 4

Ingredients

4 cups chicken stock
⅔ cup finely chopped cooked chicken
1 cup chopped broccoli
1 carrot, finely chopped
Ramen noodles (I use organic rice/millet ramen noodles)
Sea salt to taste
4 green onions, sliced

Try to top these endorsements from my grandchildren: Joel (at nine years old) said, "Grandma, I love this soup so much I wish it would turn into a person so I could marry it." Abby (at eight years old) chimed in, "Yeah, but we love everything Grandma makes."

Directions

1. In a medium soup pot, combine all ingredients except salt and green onions.
2. Bring to a boil then turn to a simmer and cook until ramen noodles are soft.
3. Add salt and green onions to serve.

Variations

1. Use beef broth with beef chunks or shreds instead of chicken.
2. Use just about any vegetable you have in the garden (zucchini, chard, spinach, etc.)
3. Make a vegetarian version with vegetable stock and drizzle in two beaten eggs when the vegetables are cooked and the broth is simmering. This is the version that elicited my grandchildren's amazing endorsements!

Sausage Vegetable Noodle Soup

How simple is this! You can vary the vegetables according to what you have available. Make this vegetarian by using vegetable stock instead of the chicken stock and beans instead of the sausage.

Servings: 2 to 3

Ingredients
    3 cups chicken stock
    4 chicken sausage links, cooked and chopped
    1 cup chopped tomatoes
    2 celery stalks, chopped
    1 carrot, chopped
    1 cup chopped spinach or Swiss chard
    1 cup chopped green cabbage
    1 teaspoon dried oregano
    1 teaspoon dried basil
    1 teaspoon dried rosemary or 2 teaspoons minced fresh rosemary
    1 teaspoon sea salt
    ¼ teaspoon cayenne pepper flakes
    2 cups cooked noodles (mini shells work great)

Directions
    1. In a large soup pot, combine all ingredients except the noodles.
    2. Simmer until vegetables are slightly soft and flavors are melded.
    3. Place desired amount of noodles in each bowl and serve the soup over the noodles.

Southwest Chicken Soup

This soup is a melody of flavors — hearty, delicious and filling. Serve with corn chips or corn muffins (see Side Dishes).

Servings: 2 to 3

Ingredients
1 tablespoon olive oil
1 small onion, chopped
2 carrots, chopped
1 bell pepper, chopped
1 small zucchini, chopped
2 cups chopped tomatoes
2 cups chopped cabbage
1 poblano pepper, roasted, seeded and diced (see Harvest Staples)
½ cup corn
1 cup cooked black beans
1 cup chopped cooked chicken
4 cups chicken broth
1 tablespoon dried oregano
1 tablespoon chili powder (optional)
Sea salt to taste

Directions
1. In a large soup pot over medium, heat olive oil.
2. Add onion, carrots, bell pepper, and zucchini and sauté until fragrant, about 5 minutes.
3. Add remaining ingredients.
4. Bring to a simmer, cover and cook about 15 to 20 minutes until vegetables are soft and flavors are melded.

Steamed Vegetable Soup

I admit, this soup is a bit plain, but it is a light, refreshing, earthy-tasting soup and works well when just a light meal is desired. It is also very easy to make.

Servings: 2 to 3

Ingredients
    3 cups of chicken or vegetable stock (or water)
    2 medium red potatoes, chopped
    2 cups chopped broccoli
    1 medium zucchini, chopped
    1 cup chopped Swiss chard or other greens
    ½ red onion, chopped
    ½ teaspoon sea salt

Directions
    1. To a soup pot, add water or stock.
    2. Insert a steamer basket.
    3. Place potatoes in the steamer basket and steam for 10 minutes.
    4. Add the remaining ingredients and steam for another 10 minutes or to desired tenderness.
    5. Combine the liquid and vegetables and purée to desired consistency.

Tomato Soup

There is nothing like a hot bowl of homemade tomato soup, for children and adults alike. Using garden tomatoes makes each bite of this soup alive with garden freshness and warm memories.

Servings: 6 to 8

Ingredients
5 pounds of tomatoes, chopped
¼ cup olive oil + 2 tablespoons
¼ cup chopped fresh basil
2 cloves garlic
¼ teaspoon cayenne pepper flakes
1 onion, chopped
2 cups chicken stock
Sea salt to taste
Herbs to taste
Grated parmesan cheese

One day, my granddaughter Abby (at 12 years old) called and I could tell she had a cold by her sniffles. She said, "Grandma, I told my caregiver what I need is some of grandma's tomato soup so I can get better." Love in a bowl of soup.

Directions
1. Heat oven to 425°F.
2. In a deep casserole dish, combine tomatoes, ¼ cup of olive oil, basil, garlic and pepper flakes.
3. Place in oven and roast for 45 minutes or until soft and cooked through.
4. In a soup pot over medium heat, heat the remaining 2 tablespoons of olive oil, add onion and cook until soft.
5. Add roasted tomato mixture and chicken stock and cook until flavors are melded, about 10 minutes.
6. Add sea salt to taste.
7. Blend until smooth.
8. Sprinkle with herbs and cheese in the serving bowl.

Vegetable Broth

I like this as much as chicken broth, and it is a great substitution to use for meatless meals. If I'm feeling cold or run down, I'll drink this in place of my cup of tea. Use it as a base in other dishes, smoothies or to cook oatmeal. It freezes well and I try to always have some on hand.

Servings: about 3½ quarts

Ingredients
    2 tablespoons olive oil
    1 leek, chopped
    1 yellow onion, chopped
    3 carrots, chopped
    3 celery stalks, chopped
    1 medium zucchini, chopped
    4 quarts water
    1 bunch parsley
    1 sprig rosemary
    1 bay leaf
    1 kombu (sea vegetable)
    Sea salt and black pepper to taste

Directions
    1. In a large stock pot over medium, heal olive oil.
    2. Add vegetables and sauté until fragrant, about 10 minutes.
    3. Add water, herbs and kombu.
    4. Bring to a boil, then lower heat and simmer for 1 hour and 30 minutes.
    5. Remove the bay leaf.
    6. Strain out vegetables, pushing out the liquid in them.
    7. The broth will last 4 to 5 days in refrigerator and freezes well.

Variations
    You can leave out any of the ingredients or add any other vegetables that you like.

Vegetable Soup

There are so many recipes for vegetable soup. Here is mine, full of garden vegetables and amazing flavor. Don't be shy with this; add as many vegetable varieties as you like.

Servings: 4 to 6

Ingredients
2 tablespoons olive oil
1 small yellow onion, chopped
2 carrots, chopped
1 red bell pepper, seeded and chopped
2 medium zucchini, chopped
½ cup sliced okra
2 tomatoes, chopped
1 quart chicken stock
½ teaspoon ground cumin
½ teaspoon turmeric
¼ teaspoon cayenne pepper
Sea salt to taste

Directions
1. In a large pot over medium, heat olive oil.
2. Add all vegetables except tomatoes and cook until fragrant, about 5 minutes.
3. Add tomatoes, chicken stock and seasonings, cover and simmer until vegetables are tender and flavors well melded, about 20 minutes.

Variations
- I've left the seasonings, except for the sea salt, out and this still tastes amazing; the flavors of the fresh garden vegetables sing a melody in one's mouth.
- Add pasta and/or cooked chickpeas, kidney beans or white beans to this to make a heartier meal.

White Bean & Vegetable Soup

This is quick and tasty. Since I prefer chicken in my soup and my husband prefers ham in his, I make the soup, chop up the amount of meat we each want, put it in the bottom of our bowls and pour the hot soup over it. Just like dining in a fancy restaurant. You can also leave the meat out and it still makes a nice soup.

Servings: 2 to 3

Ingredients

    2 tablespoons olive oil
    1 small onion, diced
    2 carrots, chopped
    2 celery stalks, chopped
    1 garlic clove, minced
    2 cups chopped tomatoes
    2 cups chopped kale, spinach or Swiss chard
    4 cups chicken or vegetable stock (or water)
    1 tablespoon minced fresh rosemary
    1 teaspoon dried thyme
    ¼ teaspoon cayenne pepper flakes
    2 cups (or 1 can) cooked white beans
    1 cup chopped cooked chicken or ham
    Sea salt and black pepper to taste

Directions

1. In a large soup pot over medium, heat olive oil.
2. Add onion, carrots, celery and garlic and sauté until fragrant, about 5 minutes.
3. Add tomatoes, greens, stock or water, herbs, salt and pepper and simmer for 20 minutes.
4. Add beans and meat (if using) and cook until well-heated.

Zucchini Soup

This is a favorite. It freezes well and is so nice to pull out on a cold winter day and enjoy a warm bowl of the garden.

Servings: 5 to 6

Ingredients
  2 tablespoons olive oil
  8 cups chopped zucchini (you can also mix in yellow squash)
  1 large onion, chopped
  3 large carrots, chopped
  4 cups chicken stock
  1 teaspoon sea salt
  Parmesan cheese

My granddaughter Abby (at five years old) was in the hospital for three months when she came down with meningitis. She was on a feeding tube for much of the time, but when the doctor was ready for her to eat regular food, we enticed her with grandma's zucchini soup and it did the trick! My zucchini soup has been famous ever since. Love in a zucchini.

Directions
1. In a large stock pot over medium-low, heat olive oil.
2. Add vegetables and sauté until fragrant, about 10 minutes.
3. Add chicken stock and salt. Cook until vegetables are tender, stirring occasionally, about 20 minutes.
4. Blend to a coarse consistency; an immersion blender works great for this.
5. Serve and sprinkle with parmesan cheese.

Variations
- Add other garden produce: spinach, Swiss chard, green beans, etc.
- Add a diced russet potato to Step 2 and rosemary and thyme to Step 3.
- The grandchildren's favorite garnish is cheddar bunny crackers.

 Salads & Dressings

Build houses and live in them;
plant gardens and eat their produce.
(Jeremiah 29:5)

One of the most beautiful signs of spring is the chives growing and blossoming. I love to sit by our chive patch and watch the bees feast on the nectar of the flowers. I'll often pick a flower or two for my salad and I'm sure I can hear the bees saying, "Hey, that's ours!"

SALADS

Beet Salad	44
Caprese	45
Carrot Salad	46
Chicken Pesto Salad	47
Chopped Salad	48
Coleslaw	49
Corn Salad	50
Cucumber Salad	51
Mixed Cabbage Blue Cheese Salad	52
Red Cabbage Salad	53
Root Veggie Shred	54
Salad Sauté	55
Tomato & Cucumber Salad	56
Zucchini Salad	57

DRESSING

Avocado Dressing	58
Creamy Dill Dressing	59
French Dressing	60
Herb Dressing	61

Beet Salad

Growing up, the only beets my mother served were the sliced beets out of a can. To me, they were just sort of a ho-hum vegetable — I didn't like or dislike them. Then as an adult I went to visit my parents one summer and my mom cooked up some beets that my dad had just harvested from the garden. I've been hooked ever since. Beets

are a staple in my garden, for both the beet tops and the beet root. The beet root stores well — long into the winter.

Servings: 3 to 4

Ingredients

    4 medium fresh beets, chopped into bite-size pieces
    ¼ cup minced fresh herbs (basil, dill, rosemary, chives)
    2 tablespoons olive oil
    Sea salt to taste

Directions

1. In a medium sauce pan add an inch of water, insert a steamer basket and place beets in the basket. Cover the pot.
2. Bring water to a gentle boil and steam beats for 20 minutes.
3. Remove from heat and mix with other ingredients.
4. Serve either hot or cold — delicious either way!

Caprese

This has to be one of the best tastes in the world. So simple. So elegant. Flavors that melt in your mouth. With the first bite I am once again sitting in a small café in northern Italy.

Servings: 2

Ingredients
  1 large tomato, sliced
  1 fresh mozzarella cheese, sliced
  ¼ cup chopped fresh basil leaves
  Sea salt
  Olive oil

Directions
  1. On a plate, arrange the tomato and cheese slices in alternate layers.
  2. Sprinkle with basil and salt.
  3. Drizzle with olive oil.

Carrot Salad

In my early years of gardening, I did not grow carrots, as I thought they were too mundane and common of a vegetable to grow. Then one year our neighbors introduced me to their garden, which was full of carrots. I had instant carrot envy! The next year I planted a row and now plant many rows each year. There is nothing like pulling a carrot out of the ground, rinsing it under the hose and munching away. Now I know why rabbits love them so much.

Don't let the simplicity of this salad fool you — it's delicious and a nice accompaniment to just about any meal.

Servings: 3 to 4

Ingredients
  6 carrots, shredded
  1 bunch green onions, chopped
  2 tablespoons olive oil
  ½ teaspoon sea salt

Directions
  Mix all ingredients together and enjoy.

Chicken Pesto Salad

I'm not a fan of mayonnaise, so using pesto to make this chicken salad is an absolutely delicious alternative and a great way to use the basil from the garden. The photo shows the salad served in Mammoth Basil leaves, which is the type of basil I like to grow.

This recipe is a great place to use the chicken I've frozen from making Chicken Stock (see Soup).

Servings: 2 to 3

Ingredients
    2 cups shredded or chopped cooked chicken
    2 celery stalks, diced
    ½ cup red onion, diced
    ½ cup fennel bulb, diced
    ¼ cup pesto (see Harvest Staples)
    Sea salt to taste

Directions
    1. Mix all ingredients together.
    2. Refrigerate until use.

Chopped Salad

This is the ultimate crunch salad. Light, refreshing and delicious. I usually leave the onion out and serve it on the side, as I have found that many people are not fond of the raw onion.

Servings: 4 to 5

Ingredients
> 2 cucumbers, diced, peeled if desired
> 1 bell pepper, diced
> 2 celery stalks, diced
> ¼ head small green cabbage, diced
> ¼ cup diced red onion
> ¼ cup diced flat leaf parsley
> 2 tablespoons olive oil
> Juice from half a lime
> Sea salt to taste

Directions
1. Mix all ingredients together.
2. If you will not be serving immediately, do not add the olive oil, lime juice and sea salt until just before serving.

Variations
- Use a poblano pepper instead of, or in addition to, the bell pepper.
- Use jalapeño or garlic-infused olive oil for the oil.

Coleslaw

For years I worked to come up with a coleslaw recipe that did not use mayonnaise. This is the outcome; it's delicious and a crowd pleaser as well. I usually put the cilantro on the side because it is one of those flavors that some people just cannot tolerate.

Servings: 7 to 8

Ingredients
    4 cups shredded green cabbage
    3 cups shredded red cabbage
    3 carrots, shredded
    6 radishes, shredded
    1 small red onion, diced
    2 jalapeño peppers, diced
    1 cup diced cilantro
    Juice of 1 lime
    ¼ cup olive oil
    1 teaspoon sea salt

Directions
    1. Combine all ingredients and mix well.
    2. Adjust lime juice, olive oil and sea salt to taste.

Corn Salad

I can't wait for the corn to ripen each year. Nothing is better than a fresh picked ear of corn on the cob smothered in butter and salt. This salad is just as pleasing!

Servings: 4 to 5

Ingredients
    3 ears raw sweet corn
    1 red bell pepper, diced
    1 poblano pepper, diced
    ½ small red onion, diced
    ¼ cup diced parsley or cilantro
    2 tablespoons fresh lime juice
    2 tablespoons olive oil
    Sea salt to taste

Directions
    1. Slice the raw corn from the cob.
    2. Mix all ingredients together, chill and serve.

I grew up on Long Island close to a farm stand that sold corn straight from the field. When my mother was serving corn on the cob, we'd go to the farm stand to buy the corn right before she was ready to cook it. I can still hear her asking the farmer, "When was this picked?" No matter what the answer was (even if it was a couple hours ago), she'd somehow convince him to go pick some corn fresh for her. She was known to eat five to six ears at a sitting, smiling the entire time. I must take after my mother.

Cucumber Salad

Who doesn't love a fresh, homegrown cucumber? Even the squirrels that live in our neighborhood can't wait for them each year. It is the crop I am saddest to see end each fall. This salad is crisp, crunchy and alive with flavor.

Servings: 3 to 4

Ingredients
2 cucumbers, quartered and sliced (peeling is optional)
1 small red onion, chopped
¼ cup chopped fresh basil leaves
2 tablespoons olive oil
Sea salt to taste

Directions
Mix all ingredients together, chill and serve.

Variation
Add some chopped fennel bulb.

Mixed Cabbage Blue Cheese Salad

One evening after picking several green and red cabbages, my husband and I were making dinner and I turned around and saw him putting this dish together. He had a moment of inspiration and we've been enjoying the results ever since. It's simple in preparation and delightful in flavor.

Servings: 3 to 4

Ingredients
> 1 cup finely chopped green cabbage
> 1 cup finely chopped red cabbage
> 1 jalapeño, diced
> ¼ cup blue cheese crumbles
> 1 tablespoon olive oil
> Sea salt to taste

Directions
> Combine all ingredients, mix and serve.

Red Cabbage Salad

This salad is beautiful with the purple, green and white vegetables. It's also full of crunch that's hard to stop eating. Don't let the turnip put you off; it's really a nice combination.

Servings: 5 to 6

Ingredients
- 1 small red cabbage (or ½ larger cabbage), shredded
- 2 cups sliced fresh snap peas (¼-inch pieces)
- 1 medium turnip, quartered and very thinly sliced
- 2 tablespoons olive oil
- Juice of 1 lime
- Sea salt to taste

Directions
1. Combine the vegetables.
2. Add the lime juice, olive oil and sea salt.
3. Mix, chill and serve.

Root Veggie Shred

This salad is a nice combination of flavors and crunch. It keeps well in the refrigerator for several days and adds a nice side to just about any dish.

Servings: 3 to 4

Ingredients
    2 medium carrots, shredded
    1 medium beet, shredded
    Equal amount of jicama, shredded
    4 green onions, diced
    2 tablespoons olive oil
    Sea salt to taste

Directions
    Combine all ingredients, chill and serve.

Salad Sauté

I make a huge tossed salad every week and eat some most days for lunch along with my turkey sandwich, or in my turkey wrap (see photo). In the winter, I like to water sauté the salad to warm it up. The first time I heard of sautéing salad, my tastes buds couldn't imagine it, but it is actually now my preferred way to eat a salad in the winter, as I need the warmth on the cold, snowy days.

Ingredients
Tossed salad with choice of ingredients
Salad dressing
Nuts or seeds of choice

Directions
1. To a medium skillet, add 2 tablespoons of water, or enough to very lightly cover the bottom.
2. Add salad and over medium heat sauté for 3 to 4 minutes, until greens are wilted and other vegetables are warmed.
3. Serve in a bowl, or as desired, and add dressing and nuts and/or seeds.

Note
There will be a small amount of water left in the skillet. Be sure to either include that in your salad or drink it separately.

Tomato & Cucumber Salad

This salad is one of the delights of summer, especially when I can pick the key ingredients right from the garden. So simple, but the flavors meld together in perfect harmony. I serve the red onion on the side since most people prefer not to have them in the salad. I usually end up eating them all, but no complaints about that!

Servings: 4

Ingredients

    2 cucumbers, peeled, quartered and sliced
    2 tomatoes, cut into large chunks
    1 small red onion, chopped
    ¼ cup chopped fresh basil
    2 tablespoons olive oil
    Sea salt to taste

Directions

    Combine all ingredients and serve.

When we lived in Denver, we had the most amazing neighbors. We both loved to garden and often pulled gardening pranks on each other. One early summer, too early for ripe tomatoes, I went out to the garden to pick a cucumber and saw two beautiful red tomatoes inside the tomato bush. Of course I rushed to pick them, not believing what I was seeing. It was the set of tomato salt and pepper shakers shown in this picture. They were put there by our neighbor, who had found them at a yard sale. It was the perfect prank, especially since I collect salt and pepper shakers.

Zucchini Salad

Zucchini is one of the first vegetables available to harvest each year (other than the greens and herbs). So this is among the first salads I make each year. Because I have been starved all winter for garden vegetables, I am sure that gives it an extra special flavor. This is a refreshing salad and a delicious way to use zucchini.

Servings: 3 to 4

Ingredients

> 1 medium zucchini, spiral shredded
> ½ cup crumbled feta cheese
> ¼ cup pine nuts
> 1 tablespoon diced fresh dill
> 1 tablespoon diced flat-leaf parsley
> 2 tablespoons olive oil
> Sea salt to taste

Directions

> Mix all ingredients, chill and serve.

Variations

> Add in some corn kernels cut fresh off the cob.

Avocado Dressing

A delicious way to combine avocado and salad dressing. It will last three to four days in the refrigerator if it doesn't disappear in the first serving!

Servings: about 2½ cups

Ingredients
> 1 large ripe avocado, pit and peel removed
> 1 cup water
> ⅓ cup olive oil
> ½ cup parsley or cilantro
> 1 large garlic clove, peeled
> Juice from half a lime
> 1 teaspoon sea salt
> Cayenne pepper to taste

Directions
> Place all items in a blender and blend until smooth.

Creamy Dill Dressing

Dill: plant it once, let it go to seed once, and you never have to plant it again. You'll have dill for the rest of your gardening life and beyond! Each spring it pops up all over the place and I just let it go. I love the smell and the taste. I give some to everyone I know. This dressing highlights dill in a simple, delicious way.

Servings: about 1½ cups

Ingredients
    1 cup plain whole milk kefir
    2 tablespoons olive oil
    1 tablespoon flax seed oil
    ¼ cup packed minced dill
    ¼ cup minced red onion
    ¼ teaspoon sea salt
    1 dash cayenne pepper

Directions
    Combine all ingredients, mix well and pour over your salad. You can never use too much of it, in my opinion.

French Dressing

I've discovered not many people like French dressing. Obviously, they haven't tasted this one. This is not the typical sweet French dressing you find in many American restaurants and store shelves; it's tangy, a bit sweet and spicy and full of flavor. I can't get enough of it and wait each year for the tomatoes to ripen so I can indulge, even though it only uses one tomato.

It freezes well, so you can make a large batch and freeze some for the winter months.

Servings: about 2 cups

Ingredients

　　1 medium tomato
　　¼ red onion
　　2 tablespoons red wine vinegar
　　1 tablespoon honey
　　1 teaspoon mustard powder
　　1 teaspoon paprika
　　½ teaspoon celery seeds
　　¼ teaspoon sea salt
　　½ cup extra virgin olive oil

Directions

1. In a blender combine all ingredients except olive oil and blend until smooth.
2. With blender running, slowly pour in the olive oil until emulsified.
3. Season to taste with salt and pepper.

Herb Dressing

This simple herb dressing is a perfect complement to a fresh garden salad. I use it liberally because it adds another layer of delicious goodness to my salad. Keep any leftover dressing in the refrigerator and use within a couple of days.

Servings: about 1½ cups

Ingredients
¾ cup of olive oil
¼ cup of apple cider or red wine vinegar
1 cup fresh herbs: any combination of oregano, dill, chives, parsley, sage, thyme, etc.

Directions
Place all ingredients in a blender and blend until smooth.

Variations and Optional Uses
- To spice the dressing up, add 1 teaspoon of powdered mustard or a clove of garlic or a sprinkle of cayenne pepper, or all of them.
- To make a creamy dressing, add some plain kefir or yogurt.
- Use the dressing on sandwiches, to dip bread in or as a chicken marinade.

🌿 Main Dishes 🌿

BEEF

You cause the grass to grow for the cattle, and plants for man to cultivate, that he may bring forth food from the earth, and wine to gladden the heart of man, oil to make his face shine, and bread to strengthen man's heart. (Psalm 104:14-15)

The recipes in the Main Dishes sections are easy-to-make, everyday meals that will put your bounty to good use while providing delicious, healthy meals. The ingredients are all readily available, if not from your garden, then from the farmers' market or the grocery store.

BBQ Beef Sandwiches	64
Beef & Okra Stew	65
Beef & Vegetable Skillet	66
Beef Stew	67
Beef Stew — Nightshade Free	68
Bratwurst in a Zucchini	69
Meatloaf	70
Shepherd's Pie	71
Spaghetti Squash with Meat Sauce	72
Spaghetti Squash Taco Pie	73
Taco Meat on Potatoes	74
Unstuffed Cabbage	75

BBQ Beef Sandwiches

Here is where having premade sauces in the freezer pays off. Serve this BBQ beef on a roll, bread, over rice, on noodles or just by itself. Your mouth will be happy no matter what way you serve it.

Servings: 4

Ingredients

> 1 pound of beef stew meat
> 1 cup of beef or vegetable stock (or water)
> 1 small onion, chopped
> 2 cups BBQ sauce (see Harvest Staples)
> 2 cups chopped cabbage

Directions

1. In a large pot combine stew meat, water or stock and onion.
2. Bring to a boil, then cover and turn to low heat. Cook for 2 to 3 hours until meat easily pulls apart. Be sure to stir occasionally and add more liquid if necessary.
3. When the meat is done, shred it with a fork.
4. Add BBQ sauce.
5. Simmer until flavors are well melded, about 20 to 30 minutes.
6. Add cabbage at the end and cook for a few minutes until slightly soft. You can also add the cabbage uncooked to the sandwich.

Beef & Okra Stew

Okra is one of those vegetables that people either love or hate. I happen to love it. At first it was a challenge to figure out how to use it in something other than fried okra. This dish highlights the okra in a very pleasing way. If you don't like okra, you can use artichoke hearts or green beans instead. Serve over noodles, rice, quinoa, bread or potatoes if desired.

Okra is a beautiful vegetable to grow. It is bush-like and adorns itself with the most beautiful flowers. Ruby Red Okra is especially stunning. It is worth growing just for the beauty of the bush and the flower.

Servings: 4 to 5

Ingredients

2 tablespoons olive oil
1 pound of stew meat
1 onion, chopped
1 clove garlic, minced
3 cups chopped tomatoes
1 pound of okra, sliced in ½-inch pieces
Sea salt to taste
Cayenne pepper to taste

Directions

1. In a large pot over medium-high, heat olive oil.
2. Add meat and brown on all sides, about 3 to 4 minutes per side.
3. Add the onions and garlic, sauté with meat until slightly soft.
4. Add tomatoes. There should be enough tomatoes to cover the meat and onions. If not, add more tomatoes or some water.
5. Bring to a boil and then cover, turn to a simmer and cook for 1 hour and 30 minutes until meat is tender. Stir occasionally and add more liquid if necessary.
6. Add okra and cook until tender, about 15 to 20 minutes.
7. Add salt and cayenne to taste.

Okra is also a lot of fun to play with!

Beef & Vegetable Skillet

This is a great one-pot meal that is quick and easy to make and a great way to use the garden kale that always seems to grow faster than I can keep up with.

Servings: 4 to 5

Ingredients
    1 pound ground beef
    1 onion, chopped
    2 cloves garlic, minced
    4 small purple or gold potatoes, diced
    1 red pepper, chopped
    1 bunch kale, stems removed, chopped
    1 cup vegetable or beef broth
    2 tablespoons chopped fresh oregano (or 1 tablespoon dried oregano)
    Sea salt to taste
    4 ounces green or black olives, sliced

Directions
    1. In a large skillet over low-medium heat, cook the ground beef until cooked through.
    2. Remove excess fat.
    3. Add remaining items, except olives.
    4. Cover and cook until potato and kale are fork tender, about 15 minutes.
    5. Add olives and cook just enough to heat.

Variations
    • Add chopped plum tomatoes.
    • Add rosemary and thyme.

Beef Stew

Stews are a delicious and filling meal, and especially enjoyable during the winter months. I often add turnips to this recipe as well. The picture shown here is from a stew I made one late January using fresh carrots, fresh turnips, frozen green beans and frozen tomatoes, all from the garden.

Servings: 4 to 5

Ingredients
1 pound stew meat
Juice of one lemon
1 cup beef stock (veggie stock or water works too)
2 cups chopped tomatoes
1 bay leaf
1 teaspoon dried basil
1 teaspoon dried thyme
¼ teaspoon cayenne pepper flakes
½ onion, diced
2 russet potatoes, chopped into bite-size pieces
3 carrots, chopped into bite-size pieces
1 cup chopped green beans

Directions
1. Marinate stew meat in the juice of one lemon overnight; this tenderizes the meat.
2. Heat oven to 300°F.
3. Drain stew meat and place in a large Dutch oven or other suitable pot.
4. Add the beef stock and tomatoes.
5. Place on the stovetop and bring to a simmer and skim off any foam that develops.
6. Add bay leaf, basil, thyme and pepper flakes.
7. Place pot in oven and simmer until the meat is very tender (about 2 to 3 hours).
8. Place pot back on stovetop and remove the bay leaf.
9. Add the remaining ingredients. Remember, the pot will be very hot!
10. Simmer for 45 to 60 minutes until vegetables are tender. Stir often to prevent sticking.

Beef Stew — Nightshade Free

This stew recipe is for those who can't, or prefer not to, eat foods in the nightshade family (such as tomatoes, potatoes, peppers), which are in the previous recipe. Don't let the sweet potato, rutabaga and parsnips shy you away, for they are a delicious combination.

Servings: 4 to 5

Ingredients
    1 pound stew meat
    Juice of one lemon
    3 cups beef stock
    1 bay leaf
    1 teaspoon dried basil
    1 teaspoon dried thyme
    1 sweet potato, chopped into bite-size pieces
    1 rutabaga, chopped into bite-size pieces
    1 large parsnip, chopped into bite-size pieces
    3 carrots, chopped into bite-size pieces
    1 leek, halved and sliced
    1 cup green beans, chopped

Directions
1. Marinate stew meat in the juice of one lemon overnight to tenderize the meat.
2. Heat oven to 300°F.
3. Drain stew meat and place in a large Dutch oven or other suitable pot.
4. Add the beef stock.
5. Place on stove and bring to a simmer. Skim off any foam that develops.
6. Add bay leaf, basil and thyme.
7. Place pot in oven and let simmer for 2 to 3 hours or until meat is very tender.
8. Place pot back on stovetop and remove the bay leaf.
9. Add the remaining ingredients. Remember, the pot will be very hot!
10. Simmer until vegetables are tender, about 45 minutes. Stir often to prevent sticking.

Bratwurst in a Zucchini

One night my husband was grilling brats for dinner and realized he didn't have any buns. Zucchini to the rescue!

Servings: 2

Ingredients
1 zucchini, slightly larger than the bratwurst
Olive oil
Sea salt
2 bratwurst

Directions
1. Fire up the grill.
2. Slice the ends off the zucchini and slice it down the center lengthwise in to two pieces. Scoop a small trench down the middle of each piece of the zucchini. This will serve to cradle the bratwurst.
3. Brush the cut side of the zucchini with olive oil and sprinkle with sea salt.
4. Place the bratwurst on the grill.
5. After about 5 minutes, place the zucchini, cut-side down, on the grill.
6. Cook until the bratwurst and zucchini are done. The zucchini will take about 10 minutes to cook if it is at room temperature when placed on the grill.
7. Serve with the bratwurst cradled in the zucchini.

Meatloaf

There are as many versions of meatloaf as there are cooks who make it. Here's mine. I serve my meatloaf with roasted butternut squash from the garden, baked potatoes or roasted root vegetables and make extra for the next day's dinner. For leftovers, slice the meatloaf and fry it up in a bit of olive oil along with leftover squash or sliced potatoes and some onions. Delicious!

Servings: 4 to 5

Ingredients
    1 egg
    1 plum tomato
    1 small onion, quartered
    1 carrot, chopped
    1 celery stalk, chopped
    1 pound of ground beef
    ½ cup breadcrumbs
    1 teaspoon sea salt
    ½ teaspoon thyme
    ½ teaspoon rosemary
    ½ teaspoon basil
    ¼ teaspoon cayenne pepper (optional)
    Ketchup or homemade tomato paste (see Harvest Staples - note that store-bought tomato paste would be too thick for the topping, but homemade works great)

Directions
    1. Heat oven to 350°F.
    2. In a blender or food processor, combine egg, tomato, onion, carrot and celery. Blend until mixed but still a bit chunky.
    3. Mix into ground beef, adding the breadcrumbs, salt and herbs.
    4. Form into a loaf shape and place in a baking dish.
    5. Top with ketchup or tomato paste.
    6. Bake for 1 hour.

Variations
    • An alternative topping is grated cheese of choice, added 10 minutes before done.
    • For grain-free meatloaf, add an extra egg and one tablespoon of coconut flour.
    • For a grain-free, egg-free meatloaf, replace the breadcrumbs and egg with ⅓ cup of oatmeal.

Shepherd's Pie

While this may not be your traditional Shepherd's Pie, it still tastes good, uses a lot of garden vegetables, and is simple to make.

Servings: 4 to 5

Ingredients

Topping:
2 pounds russet potatoes, chopped
Sea salt to taste

Filling:
1 pound ground beef
1 tablespoon tomato paste
1 leek, diced
1 celery stalk, diced
1 carrot, diced
1 cup chopped greens (spinach, Swiss chard, kale)
½ cup peas
½ cup beef or vegetable broth
1 teaspoon dried oregano
1 teaspoon dried rosemary
1 teaspoon sea salt

Instructions
1. Place potatoes in a pot, cover with water and cook until they are tender. Drain the water off the potatoes into a measuring cup. Add the cooking water back into the potatoes a bit at a time and mash to a smooth consistency. Add sea salt to taste.
2. While the potatoes are cooking, in a large skillet over low-medium heat, cook ground beef until done. Mix in the tomato paste.
3. Add remaining ingredients and cook until vegetables are slightly tender, about 10 minutes.
4. Place beef filling in the bottom of a deep dish pie pan or suitable casserole dish.
5. Cover filling with the mashed potatoes.
6. You can serve at this point or put under the broiler for a couple of minutes until topping is slightly browned.

Spaghetti Squash with Meat Sauce

This dish is how I was introduced to spaghetti squash. It's been a favorite ever since.

Servings: 4

Ingredients
    1 pound ground beef
    1 onion, chopped
    1 bell pepper, chopped
    4 cups chopped tomatoes
    ¼ cup tomato paste
    2 teaspoons dried oregano
    2 teaspoons dried basil
    ¼ teaspoon cayenne pepper flakes
    1 spaghetti squash, cooked and removed from shell (see Harvest Staples)
    1 cup grated parmesan cheese

Directions
1. Heat oven to 350°F.
2. In a pot over medium-low, cook ground beef until cooked through.
3. Remove excess fat.
4. Add onion and bell pepper and sauté until slightly tender, about 5 minutes.
5. Add remaining items except squash and cheese.
6. Cook until flavors are melded and tomatoes are cooked down, about 20 minutes.
7. Place the spaghetti squash in an oven-proof casserole dish.
8. Spoon meat sauce on top.
9. Sprinkle with cheese.
10. Bake until cheese is melted and casserole is heated through, about 20 minutes.

Variation
If both the spaghetti squash and the meat sauce are hot, you can serve by spooning the meat sauce over a mound of squash right on your plate and sprinkle with the cheese. This eliminates Steps 6 through 9.

Spaghetti Squash Taco Pie

This dish was an instant winner the first time I made it. I started out making the taco meat for burritos and was cooking a spaghetti squash to freeze at the same time. The two ended up together with delicious results. This can be a very easy dish to make with the garden harvest that is put up in the freezer — enchilada sauce, squash, peppers and corn.

Servings: 4

Ingredients

1 spaghetti squash, cooked and removed from the shell (see Harvest Staples)
1 teaspoon sea salt
1 pound ground beef
1 small onion, chopped
1 red or green bell pepper, chopped
½ cup corn kernels
1 cup enchilada sauce (see Harvest Staples)
1 cup shredded cheddar cheese

Directions

1. Heat oven to 350°F.
2. Place the spaghetti squash in the bottom of a deep pie dish and sprinkle with sea salt. You want the pie pan about half full. Depending on the size of the spaghetti squash, you may have leftover squash.
3. In a large skillet over medium-low heat, cook ground beef until cooked through.
4. Remove excess fat.
5. Add onion, pepper and corn and cook until just starting to soften, about 4 to 5 minutes.
6. Add enchilada sauce.
7. Cook until flavors are melded, about 10 minutes.
8. Place taco meat mixture over the spaghetti squash in the pie dish.
9. Sprinkle with the cheese.
10. Place in oven and bake until cheese is melted, about 10 minutes.

Taco Meat on Potatoes

You can use this taco meat in traditional taco shells, corn or flour tortillas too. It freezes well and is nice to have on hand for nights when you don't have time to cook and just want to pull something out of the freezer.

Servings: 4 to 5

Ingredients
    1 russet potato for each person
    1 pound ground beef
    1 small onion, chopped
    1 bell pepper, chopped
    1 cup enchilada sauce (see Harvest Staples)
    Sea salt to taste
    Optional toppings: grated cheese, sour cream, guacamole

Directions
    1. Heat oven to 350°F.
    2. Wash potatoes, puncture with a fork in a couple of places and bake until soft, about 1 hour. Alternatively, you can slice the potatoes and steam them until tender.
    3. In a large skillet over medium-low heat, cook ground beef until cooked through.
    4. Remove excess fat.
    5. Add onion and pepper and cook until just soft, about 5 minutes.
    6. Add enchilada sauce and cook until heated and flavors are melded, about 10 minutes.
    7. Season with salt.
    8. Slice potatoes in half and cover with the taco meat, or serve over the sliced, steamed potatoes.
    9. Add optional toppings, if desired.

Unstuffed Cabbage

I make this dish with homegrown tomatoes, tomato paste, green pepper, cabbage and cayenne pepper. Even long after the gardening season is over I can make it with tomatoes and peppers that I've put up in the freezer and it is still bursting with flavor!

Servings: 4

Ingredients

1 pound ground beef
1 onion, diced
1 green bell pepper, diced
4 cups chopped tomatoes
3 tablespoon tomato paste
2 tablespoons chopped fresh herbs (oregano, basil, parsley)
1 teaspoon sea salt
¼ teaspoon cayenne pepper flakes
4 cups chopped cabbage
Cooked noodles of choice

One of my mother's often-cooked dishes was stuffed cabbage; it was something the entire family loved. One day I was craving my mother's stuffed cabbage, but making it seemed like too much work, and that is how this dish was born. The ingredients are the same as my mother's, but the presentation is different. It has become one of our favorite dishes.

Directions

1. In a large pot over medium-low, cook ground beef until cooked through.
2. Remove excess fat.
3. Add onion and bell pepper and cook for a minute or two.
4. Add remaining ingredients except cabbage and noodles.
5. Cook until tomatoes are cooked down and flavors melded, about 30 minutes.
6. Add cabbage, mix and cook for 5 minutes (don't overcook).
7. Serve over noodles.

Main Dishes

POULTRY

*For I was hungry and you gave me food, I was thirsty and you
gave me drink, I was a stranger and you welcomed me.*
(Matthew 25:35)

BBQ Chicken Sandwiches	78
Chicken Cakes	79
Chicken & Cauliflower Pasta	80
Chicken Fajitas	81
Chicken Fried Rice	82
Chicken Skillet	83
Chicken Taquitos	84
Millet Skillet	86
Pasta with Pesto & Chicken	87
Pesto Pizza with Chicken	88
Quinoa with Chicken & Vegetables	89
Southwest Spaghetti Squash	90
Southwest Stew	91
Spring Pasta	93
Turkey Sandwich — 5 Ways	94
Turnip Sausage Skillet	96

BBQ Chicken Sandwiches

I eat this with or without the bread along with a couple of pickles and whatever vegetables I have around. It also tastes delicious on top of cooked spaghetti squash (see Harvest Staples). With the BBQ sauce premade, it is a quick and delicious meal.

Servings: 4

Ingredients
    3 cups shredded cooked chicken
    2 cups BBQ sauce (see Harvest Staples)
    Sea salt to taste
    Bread or buns of choice
    2 cups shredded green cabbage

Directions
    1. In a medium saucepan combine chicken and BBQ sauce.
    2. Simmer covered until well heated, about 15 to 20 minutes.
    3. Salt to taste.
    4. Serve on buns, bread of choice, spaghetti squash or noodles.
    5. Layer shredded cabbage on top of chicken.

Variation
    Alternatively, you can make this in a slow cooker as follows:
    1. Slice an onion and put it in the bottom of the slow cooker.
    2. Brown 2 chicken breasts in olive oil on the stove for 3 to 4 minutes per side.
    3. Place the chicken on top of the onions.
    4. Pour in the BBQ sauce.
    5. Cook on low for 4 hours.
    6. Shred chicken.

Chicken Cakes

These are a great accompaniment to a salad or other garden vegetables. They freeze well and I like to have some on hand to grab for a lunch to go. I often make these when I make chicken stock (see Soup), using the meat stripped from the bones. They freeze well.

Servings: 8 patties

Ingredients

    2 cups chopped cooked chicken
    2 eggs, beaten
    1 cup breadcrumbs
    1 cup chopped onion
    1 cup chopped celery
    ¼ cup chopped parsley
    2 teaspoons sea salt
    1 teaspoon black pepper
    Olive oil or coconut oil for cooking the cakes

Directions

1. Place all ingredients except oil in a food processor and blend to a chunky consistency.
2. Mold into patties, ⅓ of a cup each.
3. Heat 2 tablespoons oil in frying pan and cook the cakes over medium heat until golden brown on both sides and cooked through, about 5 to 7 minutes on each side. Add more oil as needed.

Chicken & Cauliflower Pasta

I learned this dish from an Italian friend of mine. She taught me to make it with broccoli, but it is delicious with cauliflower too. Although it seems like an odd combination and is mono colored, I've had friends ask me for the recipe after eating it. Don't be afraid of the cayenne; it gives the dish an additional layer of flavor.

Servings: 4

Ingredients
    2 cups small pasta shells
    1 cauliflower, cut into florets
    1 tablespoon olive oil
    1 pound chicken breast, diced
    1 medium red onion, diced
    2 tablespoons butter
    Sea salt to taste
    Cayenne pepper to taste
    Parmesan cheese, freshly grated

Directions
    1. Cook shells according to instructions and set aside.
    2. Steam the cauliflower until tender. Using the back of a fork or a potato masher, break up the cauliflower florets into small pieces.
    3. In a large skillet over medium, heat olive oil.
    4. Add chicken and sauté until cooked through.
    5. Add the onion and cook until tender.
    6. Add the cauliflower, noodles and butter. Mix well and heat through.
    7. Salt to taste.
    8. Sprinkle with cayenne pepper.
    9. Serve with grated parmesan cheese.

Tip
    To prevent using an extra pot, bring the water for the noodles to a boil and add the cauliflower. Cook until the cauliflower is tender and use a slotted spoon to remove the cauliflower from the water. Then add the noodles to the same water and cook as usual.

Chicken Fajitas

This is one of my favorite make-for-company dishes. Serve the fajitas wrapped in tortillas or on top of rice and cover with tomatillo sauce (see Harvest Staples) and it's a winner every time.

Servings: 4

Ingredients
1 pound chicken breast, sliced into bite-size strips
3 tablespoons fajita seasoning*
Olive oil for cooking
6 bell peppers (mixed colors), stem and seeds removed and sliced
2 poblano peppers, stem and seeds removed and chopped
1 red onion, peeled and sliced
1 medium zucchini, cut into thick matchsticks
1 medium yellow squash, cut into thick matchsticks
Tortillas of choice
2 cups tomatillo sauce (see Harvest Staples)

Directions
1. Toss the sliced chicken in the fajita seasoning.
2. In a large skillet over medium, heat a small amount of olive oil. Add chicken and cook until cooked through.
3. Remove chicken from the pan and set aside.
4. Add peppers, onion, zucchini and yellow squash. Cook until slightly tender, about 5 minutes.
5. Add chicken back into pan and mix well.
6. Place desired amount in a tortilla or on rice and top with tomatillo sauce.

* You can buy fajita seasoning premade or make your own. Here is my recipe. I make up a batch and keep it in a jar in my pantry for quick access. Combine all spices and mix well.

¼ cup chili powder	1 tablespoon onion powder
2 tablespoons sea salt	2 teaspoons garlic powder
2 tablespoons cumin	½ teaspoon cayenne pepper
2 tablespoons paprika	

Chicken Fried Rice

This is such an easy dish to make, especially if you have some chicken in the freezer and some leftover brown rice.

Servings: 2

Ingredients
    1 tablespoon olive oil
    2 cups diced vegetables (red onion, carrots, zucchini, broccoli, spinach, etc.)
    1 cup diced cooked chicken
    2 cups cooked brown rice
    1 tablespoon minced fresh parsley (or 1 teaspoon dried)
    1 tablespoon minced fresh chives (or 1 teaspoon dried)
    2 tablespoon sunflower seeds (optional)
    Sea salt to taste

Directions
    1. In a large skillet over medium, heat olive oil.
    2. Add vegetables and sauté until just tender.
    3. Add the chicken and rice and cook until heated through.
    4. Add herbs and salt.
    5. Garnish with sunflower seeds and serve.

Chicken Skillet

This is a quick and easy meal that is nutritious and delicious. You can be creative with the vegetables and amounts you add based on what is in your garden or refrigerator; it's a very flexible dish.

Servings: 4 to 6

Ingredients

2 tablespoons olive oil
1 onion, chopped
2 chicken breasts, cut into small medallions
1 garlic clove, minced
2 tablespoons olive oil
1 cup chicken stock
3 cups chopped kale, stems removed (Swiss chard or spinach work too)
2 potatoes or turnips, chopped
2 tomatoes, diced
1 zucchini, chopped
1 carrot, chopped
2 tablespoons diced fresh herbs (rosemary, oregano, sage, thyme)
¼ teaspoon cayenne pepper flakes
Sea salt to taste

Directions

1. In a large deep skillet over medium, heat olive oil.
2. Add onion and sauté until it starts to soften.
3. Add chicken and garlic. Brown and cook chicken through.
4. Add chicken stock and then the remaining ingredients to the skillet.
5. Simmer until chicken and vegetables are cooked.
6. Serve in bowls.

Chicken Taquitos

There may not be many garden vegetables in this recipe, but dip these in homemade salsa (see Side Dishes) and you've got plenty of vegetables. Serve this with Spanish rice (see Side Dishes) and it's a perfect meal.

Servings: 12 taquitos

Ingredients

  2 tablespoons olive oil, plus more for cooking tortillas
  1 small onion, diced
  2 garlic cloves, minced
  2 jalapeños or 1 poblano, diced
  2 cups finely shredded cooked chicken
  1 teaspoon cumin
  Sea salt and black pepper to taste
  ½ cup grated cheese of choice (optional)
  12 corn tortillas (I use sprouted, organic corn tortillas)
  Salsa (see Side Dishes)

We moved to southern California when I was nine years old and I quickly developed a love for Mexican food. Taquitos were a favorite. When I moved to Colorado in my 30s, for some reason I forgot all about them. Then one day in my late 50s I saw an ad in a paper for frozen taquitos, and my taste buds would not settle down until I had one. After a couple of weeks of ruminating on taquitos, I decided that if a frozen food factory could make them, so could I. I was delighted at my first try and now I can enjoy them again.

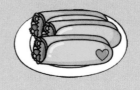

Chicken Taquitos continued

Directions
1. Heat oven to 350°F.
2. In a skillet over medium, heat olive oil.
3. Add onion, garlic, jalapeño or poblano and sauté until soft, about 5 minutes.
4. Add chicken and cumin, salt and pepper and cook until heated.
5. The filling is now ready for the tortillas. Remove from heat and set aside.
6. In a small skillet, add one tablespoon olive oil and heat over medium-high heat.
7. Add one corn tortilla at a time and cook for 10 seconds on each side until just soft and pliable. Add more oil if needed.
8. Add filling in row in middle of each tortilla.
9. Sprinkle with cheese, if using.
10. Roll tortilla up tightly and place rolled end-down on a baking sheet.
11. Place in oven and bake for 25 to 30 minutes until golden brown.
12. Sprinkle with sea salt.
13. Serve with salsa.

Millet Skillet

I eat this for breakfast, lunch or dinner — it's great for any meal. It can be made vegan by leaving out the sausage and adding more nuts, seeds or tofu (or nothing). The vegetables can also be changed up. I enjoy this right from the skillet; it keeps it warm while I am eating it and reduces the number of dishes I have to wash (my husband taught me this from his bachelor days).

Servings: 1

Ingredients
¼ cup of water
2 chicken or turkey sausages
3 Brussels sprouts, diced (or other veggie)
1 cup diced greens (dandelion, spinach, etc.)
1½ cup cooked millet*
1 tablespoon sunflower seeds
Sea salt and herbs to taste

Directions
1. To a small skillet, add water, sausage, Brussels sprouts and greens. Cover and simmer until sausage is cooked and vegetables are tender, about 6 to 7 minutes.
2. Dice the sausage.
3. Add millet and cook until heated. Millet is a somewhat dry grain, so add more water if necessary.
4. Remove from stove and add sunflower seeds, sea salt and herbs.

* To cook the millet: rinse 1 cup of dry millet under running water. To a medium saucepan, add the rinsed millet and 2 cups of water. Bring to a boil, then turn down to a very low simmer. Cover and cook for 15 to 20 minutes until the water is absorbed. This yields 4 cups of cooked millet. I use the extra millet over the next several days or freeze it.

Pasta with Pesto & Chicken

Pasta with pesto served as a side dish is the traditional use for pesto and that is how I learned to love it. I add chicken and vegetables to make a one-dish meal. Of course, while I'm eating it, I'm smiling and thinking of the garden with the basil and squash growing, the harvesting, making the pesto and of my times in Italy eating pasta with pesto. It is that unseen ingredient (love) that once again makes a dish shine.

Servings: 4

Ingredients
>   2 cups dry pasta (shells, rotini, penne, etc.) or 8 ounces dry spaghetti
>   2 tablespoons olive oil
>   3 cups chopped zucchini and yellow squash mix
>   2 cups diced cooked chicken (leftover grilled or roasted chicken works great)
>   ½ cup pesto (see Harvest Staples)
>   Parmesan cheese and pine nuts for serving

Directions
1. Follow directions on package to cook pasta. Drain and set aside when it is done.
2. In a large sauce pan over medium, heat the olive oil.
3. Add the squash mix and sauté until just starting to get tender, about 3 to 4 minutes.
4. Add the chicken and cook until heated.
5. Add the cooked pasta and mix in well. When all ingredients are heated, turn off the heat.
6. Add pesto and mix well.
7. Serve with parmesan cheese and pine nuts sprinkled on top.

Variation
>   If you do not have cooked chicken, use 1 pound of uncooked chicken, chopped into bite-size pieces. In a saucepan over medium, heat 1 tablespoon of olive oil. Add chicken and sauté until cooked through.

Pesto Pizza with Chicken

YUM! Need I say anything else?

Servings: 2

Ingredients

1 large pizza crust
½ cup pesto (see Harvest Staples)
1 cup diced cooked chicken
¼ cup diced red onion
½ cup grated parmesan
Arugula, thinly sliced
Red pepper flakes

Directions

1. Heat oven to 350°F.
2. Mix 1 tablespoon of the pesto with the chicken.
3. Spread the remaining pesto on the pizza crust.
4. Spread the chicken evenly on the crust.
5. Sprinkle on the red onion.
6. Sprinkle on the cheese.
7. Bake for 15 to 20 minutes until cheese is melted and crust is lightly browned.
8. Sprinkle with arugula and red pepper flakes.
9. Cut and serve.

Variations

- Use cooked, chopped sausage instead of chicken.
- Add chopped tomatoes.
- Add chopped artichoke hearts.

Quinoa with Chicken & Vegetables

This is a quick and easy one-pot meal. You can also make this meal vegetarian (and vegan) by leaving out the chicken and adding in black beans (see Quinoa with Beans & Vegetables in Main Dishes - Vegetarian).

Servings: 4

Ingredients

    1 cup quinoa
    2 cups water, vegetable or chicken broth
    1 cup finely chopped cooked chicken
    ¼ cup finely chopped onion
    2 cloves of garlic, minced
    1½ cups finely chopped seasonal vegetables (zucchini, asparagus, corn, spinach, chard, etc.)
    1 tablespoon dried basil
    1 tablespoon dried thyme
    1 tablespoon dried oregano
    ½ teaspoon sea salt

Directions

1. Rinse quinoa in cold water.
2. In a large skillet combine all ingredients. Mix well.
3. Bring to a boil.
4. Lower heat to a simmer, cover and cook for 20 minutes or until the liquid is absorbed.

Southwest Spaghetti Squash

I'm always looking for new ways to enjoy the bounty of spaghetti squash. Of course, I never tire of eating it with butter, salt and chives, but it's nice to make a full meal of it and enjoy it in a variety of dishes. This one is fresh, light and delicious.

You can leave the chicken out and serve this as a side dish with grilled chicken or as a vegetarian meal.

Servings: 4

Ingredients
    1 pound chicken breast, cut into bite-size pieces
    2 tablespoons fajita seasoning (see Chicken Fajitas in this chapter)
    1 tablespoon olive oil
    1 small red onion, chopped
    1 red bell pepper, chopped
    1 cup corn kernels
    2 cups chopped spinach
    2 poblano peppers (roasted or fresh), diced
    2 cups chopped tomatoes
    1 cup cooked black beans
    1 medium spaghetti squash, cooked and removed from the shell (see Harvest Staples)
    Sea salt to taste

Directions
    1. Combine chicken and fajita seasoning.
    2. In a large skillet over medium, heat olive oil.
    3. Add chicken and cook until done.
    4. Add onion and bell pepper and cook until just tender.
    5. Add corn, spinach, poblano peppers, tomatoes, black beans and salt. Cook until warmed and spinach is wilted.
    6. Mix in spaghetti squash and cook until heated through.
    7. Add sea salt.

Southwest Stew

This recipe is a favorite in our home. I add only sea salt because I enjoy the layers of flavor without additional spices. My husband adds some chili powder in his bowl for an extra kick.

Servings: 4

Ingredients

1 tablespoon olive oil
1 pound chicken, cut into bite-size pieces (you can also use ground chicken or turkey)
4 cups chicken stock
1 butternut squash, chopped into bite-size pieces
2 carrots, chopped
2 golden or purple potatoes, chopped
2 poblano peppers, roasted, peeled, seeded and diced (see Harvest Staples)
1 green bell pepper, chopped
1 teaspoon sea salt
1 tablespoon chili powder (optional)
1 teaspoon cumin (optional)
1 medium zucchini, chopped

Directions

1. In a large soup pot over medium, heat olive oil.
2. Add chicken and sauté until cooked.
3. Add all ingredients except zucchini.
4. Cover and simmer until squash and potato are almost tender, about 20 minutes.
5. Add zucchini and cook until all vegetables are tender.

Variations

- Add turnips, rutabagas or sweet potatoes.
- Add garden greens (spinach, kale, Swiss chard).
- Use cooked chicken and place all ingredients in the pot and cook from Step 3 forward.

Spring Pasta

One of the highlights of spring is foraging for wild asparagus along the wilderness trail where we walk. It's hard to find and is only there for a couple of weeks each spring, but finding it is like finding a treasure. Eating the freshly picked, raw asparagus makes enduring the winter bearable (almost)!

Servings: 2

Ingredients
2 cups dry pasta of choice
2 tablespoons olive oil
1½ cups chopped asparagus
2 cups chopped spinach
1 cup diced cooked chicken
¼ teaspoon ground cayenne pepper
1 tablespoon butter
Sea salt to taste
Parmesan cheese
Pine nuts

Directions
1. Cook pasta according to instructions and set aside.
2. In a large skillet over medium-low, heat olive oil.
3. Add asparagus and cook until slightly tender.
4. Add spinach and cook until wilted.
5. Add chicken, cayenne pepper, butter and salt and cooked pasta.
6. Mix to coat and heat ingredients.
7. Serve topped with parmesan cheese and pine nuts.

Turkey Sandwich — 5 Ways

I eat a turkey sandwich, or some form thereof, almost every day for lunch. Even if I have a big salad, I have a turkey sandwich too. Here are some ways I keep the sandwich interesting.

We were having a picnic one day with grandson Ruben Jr. (at eight years old). I asked him how he liked his turkey sandwich (the plain version) and this was his response: "It's amazing; it's from God, it's from love! It's awesome!" Guess he liked it.

Servings: 1

Turkey Sandwich Plain
    2 pieces of bread (or a bagel), toasted
    2–3 slices of turkey
    Chimichurri or pesto sauce (see Harvest Staples)
    Garden greens and chives
    Cayenne pepper
    Coarse sea salt

Toast the bread, spread it with the desired sauce and place the remaining ingredients.

Turkey Sandwich Grilled with Pickles
    2 pieces of bread
    Butter
    2 slices of turkey
    1 slice of cheese
    Dill pickles, sliced flat

Butter one side of each slice of bread, place the turkey and cheese between the unbuttered sides, grill until bread is browned and cheese melted. Open the sandwich and add the pickles.

Turkey Sandwich Mediterranean Style

    Olive oil
    Coarse sea salt
    2 pieces of bread
    Pesto (see Harvest Staples)
    2 slices of turkey
    1 artichoke heart, chopped
    Grated parmesan cheese

94

Turkey Sandwich — continued

Coat a small frying pan with olive oil and sprinkle the salt on the olive oil. Spread the inside of the bread with pesto, place the turkey on the bread, add the artichoke heart and sprinkle with parmesan cheese. Heat the frying pan over low-medium heat and place the sandwich in the pan. Grill on each side until crispy and brown.

Turkey Spice Tortillas

    2 tablespoons olive oil
    Sprinkle of turmeric, cumin, coriander, cayenne
    Salad greens, chopped
    Radishes, chopped
    Turkey slices, chopped
    2 small tortillas of choice (I use cassava)
    Chives

In a small frying pan, heat olive oil. Add spices and mix. Add greens and radishes, sauté until warmed and slightly wilted. Add turkey. Mix well. Add mixture to the tortillas, sprinkle with chives and roll.

Turkey and Salad Wrap

    1 large wrap of choice
    Sliced turkey
    Salad with vegetables of choice
    Salad dressing of choice (see Harvest Staples and Salads & Dressings)
    Chives (with flowers if available), chopped
    Pumpkin seeds (or seeds of choice)

Add dressing to salad and mix. Lay turkey on wrap and top with salad, sprinkle with chives and roll. In the winter I warm the wrap in a frying pan and then sauté the salad so it's warm (see Salad Sauté in Salads & Dressings).

Turnip Sausage Skillet

One hot July day, I was pondering a pile of just harvested turnips, imagining what could be, and this is what turned up for dinner that night.

Servings: 2

Ingredients
>   2 tablespoons olive oil
>   3 medium turnips, peeled and diced into ½-inch cubes
>   4 breakfast sausages of choice
>   ¼ cup diced red onion
>   2 cups chopped seasonal vegetables
>   Handful of chopped fresh herbs
>   Sprinkle of cayenne pepper

Directions
1. In a large skillet over medium, heat olive oil.
2. Add turnips and sausages, cover, and cook for 7 minutes or until sausages are cooked and turnips are almost done (semi-soft).
3. Add onions and vegetables, cover, and cook until turnips and vegetables are cooked.
4. Add herbs, sprinkle with cayenne pepper and cut sausage into bite-size pieces.

🌿 **Main Dishes** 🌿

VEGETARIAN

Yet he did not leave himself without witness,
for he did good by giving you rains from heaven and fruitful
seasons, satisfying your hearts with food and gladness.
(Acts 14:17)

Avocado Toast with Fried Tofu	98
Black Bean Skillet	99
Black Bean Tostadas	100
Eggs Poblano	101
Frittata	102
Mung Dal & Basmati Rice	104
Pizza with Tofu	106
Pumpkin Cream of Buckwheat	107
Quinoa with Beans & Vegetables	108
Ratatouille	109
Spring Rolls with Fried Tofu	110
Spaghetti Squash Quinoa Fritters	112
Summer Spaghetti	114
Swiss Chard Cakes	115
Tofu & Vegetable Fried Rice	116
Veggie & Bean Tacos	117
Zucchini Fritters	118

Avocado Toast with Fried Tofu

Here's my version of avocado toast. It's a favorite for meatless Fridays and hot summer days.

The little green watermelon-looking vegetables in the picture are Mexican Sour Gherkin Cucumbers. They look like tiny watermelons and taste like tiny cucumbers. They are easy to grow, delicious, and very rarely make it all the way into the house when I'm picking them.

Servings: 1

Ingredients
    1 slice of bread, toasted
    ½ avocado
    Sea salt to taste
    Cayenne pepper to taste
    1 thick slice of garden tomato
    Garden greens of choice
    2 slices of fried tofu (see Spring Rolls with Tofu in this chapter)

Directions
    1. Spread avocado on the toast.
    2. Sprinkle with sea salt and cayenne.
    3. Place the tomato, greens and tofu on top.

Black Bean Skillet

One end-of-garden-season day, I was looking in the refrigerator for some-thing to make for a meatless lunch. What I found was half a yellow squash, a poblano pepper, and a few sprigs of cilantro, all the last of their class for the season — just a few rem-nants. Plus a cup of leftover black beans. Before you know it, this recipe was born. In the photo, I've used red cabbage, Brussels sprouts, red pepper and yellow squash. It's an easy and satisfying meal.

Servings: 1 main or 2 side

Ingredients
1 tablespoon olive oil
¼ cup diced onion
1 cup chopped vegetables
1 poblano pepper, chopped (you can also use an Anaheim or bell pepper)
1 cup cooked black beans
1 slice of pepper jack cheese, chopped
Fresh cilantro, chopped
Sea salt

Directions
1. In a small skillet over medium, heat olive oil.
2. Add onion and sauté until soft.
3. Add vegetables and pepper and cook to desired softness.
4. Add beans and cook until heated through.
5. Sprinkle with cheese, cilantro and sea salt.

Variations
- Add some shredded chicken.
- This can be eaten cold as a salad as well.

Black Bean Tostadas

These make for a simple, delicious meal. Use whatever toppings you like — roasted vegetables, cheese and additional spices go well with these.

Servings: 2 to 3

Ingredients
    6 corn tortillas
    Olive oil to brush on tortillas
    Sea salt to sprinkle on tortillas
    1 tablespoon olive oil
    ½ cup diced red onion
    ½ red bell pepper, diced
    1 teaspoon chili powder
    1 teaspoon cumin powder
    ½ teaspoon sea salt
    2 cups (or 1 can) cooked black beans
    ½ cup water
    2 cups shredded cabbage
    1 tomato, chopped
    1 avocado, chopped
    Salsa (see Side Dishes)

Directions
1. To cook the tortillas:
    a. Heat oven to 400°F.
    b. Brush each side of tortilla with olive oil.
    c. Place on a baking sheet, bake for 5 minutes, turn, bake for another 5 minutes or until tortillas are crisp and brown.
    d. Remove from oven and sprinkle with sea salt while still hot. Set aside.
2. To cook the beans:
    a. In a medium skillet over medium, heat 1 tablespoon olive oil.
    b. Add onion and pepper and sauté until soft, about 5 minutes.
    c. Add chili powder, cumin and sea salt. Stir until mixed.
    d. Add beans and water. Cook until heated and flavors are melded, about 10 minutes.
    e. Lightly mash beans or briefly blend in a blender, adding more liquid if necessary.
3. Assemble:
    a. Spread beans on tortilla.
    b. Add cabbage, tomato, avocado and salsa as toppings.

Eggs Poblano

This is my husband's favorite dish to make when he's on his own for dinner or when we each decide to make our own dinner. It has been a staple for him since his college days when a dozen eggs and an eight-pack of burger buns were 29 cents each.

Servings: 1

Ingredients
2 English muffins or hamburger buns
Butter
½ poblano pepper, diced
2 eggs
2 slices of cheddar cheese (or cheese of choice)

Directions
1. Spread butter on muffins or buns.
2. To a large skillet over medium, add the muffins or buns buttered side down. Cook until browned and heated through. Remove from pan and place on a plate in a warmed oven.
3. Add a tablespoon of butter to the pan and slightly brown.
4. Add the poblano peppers.
5. Crack the eggs open over the peppers in the frying pan and break the yokes with the edge of a spatula.
6. Cook until egg whites are cooked through, flip eggs with imbedded peppers over.
7. Cook another minute or so, then place cheese on top of eggs.
8. Turn off heat.
9. Put the eggs on the muffins/buns and serve.

Variation
Add a slice of ham, Canadian bacon or bacon.

Frittata

We often forego meat on Fridays and this is one of our favorite go-to dinners. It's a simple, light and delicious meal and any leftover frittata makes a great breakfast or lunch the next day. It can be made with just about any combination of vegetables.

Servings: 4

Ingredients

    3 tablespoons coconut oil, divided
    1 cup grated or diced potatoes (or frozen hash browns)
    4 cups chopped vegetables
    6 large eggs
    ¼ cup diced fresh herbs
    Sea salt to taste

Directions

1. In a large skillet over medium, heat 1 tablespoon of coconut oil.
2. Add potatoes and cook for several minutes until soft.
3. Add remaining vegetables to skillet and cook to barely tender.
4. While potato and vegetable mixture is cooking, to a 10-inch skillet add remaining coconut oil and heat over very low heat. Make sure coconut oil is spread evenly over bottom of skillet.
5. In a medium bowl, whisk eggs until smooth.

Frittata continued

6. To the whisked eggs, add cooked potato with vegetables, herbs and salt and mix with a spoon.
7. Pour mixture into the heated 10-inch skillet and cover. Cook mixture over low heat until cooked through, about 20 minutes, rotate skillet occasionally to be sure it heats evenly.
8. When the frittata is cooked, place it under the oven broiler for a minute or two to heat and brown the top.
9. Loosen frittata from the skillet with a flexible spatula and slide frittata out of pan onto a serving plate. Cut and serve.

Variations

Here are some favorite combinations:
- Leeks and artichoke hearts.
- Zucchini, yellow squash, red onion.
- Zucchini, red pepper, chili pepper (Anaheim, poblano, jalapeño).
- Add some grated cheese to the top before broiling.

Mung Dal & Basmati Rice

This recipe is based on the Ayurvedic Kitchari recipe. I can't claim it for my own, but I have adjusted it to how I like it. It's a breakfast staple, but is good anytime of the day. It will last in the refrigerator for several days so you can enjoy it on successive days. It also freezes well.

Servings: 4

Ingredients
    ½ cup basmati rice
    ½ cup yellow split mung dal
    1 teaspoon apple cider vinegar
    1 tablespoon coconut oil or ghee
    2 tablespoons grated fresh ginger
    1 teaspoon turmeric (or 2 tablespoons fresh grated)
    1 teaspoon sea salt
    ½ teaspoon cardamom pods
    ½ teaspoon mustard seeds
    3 cups water
    2 cups chopped vegetables

Mung Dal & Basmati Rice continued

Directions
1. Mix mung dal and rice together and rinse well.
2. Add to a bowl and cover with 3 to 4 cups of water, add apple cider vinegar, mix and soak overnight.
3. Drain and rinse mung dal and rice.
4. In a medium saucepan over medium heat, melt coconut oil.
5. Add spices and cook for a minute until aromatic.
6. Add mung dal, rice and water; mix well.
7. Bring to a boil, then turn to a very low heat and cover.
8. Cook for 15 minutes, stirring occasionally.
9. Add vegetables, mix well and bring back to a simmer.
10. Lower heat, cover and cook for another 15 minutes or until all moisture is absorbed.

Variations
Some favorite vegetable combinations:
- Eggplant, greens (beet, Swiss chard, kale, spinach) and carrots.
- Brussels sprouts, carrots, greens.
- Green beans, carrots, peas.
- Broccoli, zucchini, carrots.

Pizza with Tofu

A bit odd maybe, but quite good. My husband wanted pepperoni pizza and I felt like having tofu, so we each took half of the crust. We were both happy with the results. This recipe is for a full, individual size nine-inch pizza. It also works for half of a larger crust, as shown in the photo.

Servings: 1

Ingredients

    ½ cup diced organic firm tofu
    1 tablespoon olive oil
    Seasonings to taste for tofu: garlic powder, onion powder, cayenne pepper
    1 individual size 9-inch pizza crust
    ¼ cup pesto of choice (see Harvest Staples)
    2 tablespoons diced red onion
    ¼ cup diced poblano pepper (or pepper of choice)
    ¼ cup diced olives of choice
    ⅓ cup grated parmesan cheese
    Oregano to taste, fresh or dried

Directions

1. Heat oven to 350°F.
2. Before dicing the tofu, squeeze it between a towel to remove excess water.
3. In a small skillet, heat olive oil over medium heat. Add tofu, sprinkle with seasonings, and cook until lightly browned. Remove from heat.
4. On the pizza crust, spread the pesto.
5. Add tofu and remaining ingredients, spreading out evenly.
6. Bake until cheese is melted and crust is lightly browned, about 20 minutes.

Pumpkin Cream of Buckwheat

This came about because I had just a small amount of pumpkin left over and a small amount of molasses and did not want either to go to waste. So, lying awake in the middle of the night, I was pondering what to do with these two items and what to have for breakfast. Need I say more? It is now a favorite winter breakfast.

Servings: 1 (easily doubles)

Ingredients
  1¼ cups water
  ¼ teaspoon sea salt
  ¼ cup cream of buckwheat
  2 tablespoons pumpkin purée
  2 tablespoons pumpkin seeds
  2 teaspoons molasses
  ½ cup milk of choice (dairy, almond, etc.)
  ¼ cup nuts/seeds of choice

Directions
1. In a small saucepan, add water and sea salt and bring to a boil.
2. Add cream of buckwheat.
3. Turn heat down and simmer until most of the water is absorbed.
4. Add pumpkin and cook for another couple of minutes until the pumpkin is heated and well mixed in.
5. Place cooked cereal in a bowl.
6. Add pumpkin seeds.
7. Add molasses.
8. Serve with the milk and nuts/seeds.

Variations
- Use real maple syrup in place of the molasses (or both!).
- Add grated turmeric.
- Sprinkle with cinnamon.
- Replace the pumpkin with half of a diced apple or ½ cup diced rhubarb. Add these in at Step 1 so they cook along with water and buckwheat.
- Follow my husband's advice and save yourself cleaning a bowl and eat your cereal right out of the pan.

Quinoa with Beans & Vegetables

This is a quick and easy dish to make. You can add shredded or chopped chicken too (see Quinoa with Chicken and Vegetables in Main Dishes - Poultry). The key to this dish is to chop the vegetables very small.

Servings: 4

Ingredients

1 cup quinoa
1 cup cooked beans (black, red, adzuki, pinto)
1 small leek, finely chopped
1 cup finely chopped greens (spinach, chard, kale)
1 cup chopped tomato
½ cup corn kernels
1 small zucchini or yellow squash, diced
1 poblano pepper, seeded and diced
1 tablespoon each dried basil, parsley, oregano, or any combo of dried or fresh herbs
1 teaspoon sea salt
2 cups water (or chicken, vegetable stock)*

*If tomato is juicy, decrease liquid slightly to compensate

Directions

1. Rinse quinoa well.
2. In a large skillet, combine all ingredients and mix.
3. Bring to a boil.
4. Turn to a simmer, cover and cook for 20 minutes or until all liquid is absorbed.

Variations

- You can also make this much like you would fried rice — sauté the vegetables in olive oil until soft, add cooked quinoa and heat through.
- Change up the vegetables. You want about 3 cups total, give or take.

Ratatouille

The first time I made this dish I thought my taste buds were going to pop, the flavor of all the freshly picked garden vegetables exploded in my mouth. After a couple bites my husband said, "Dear, are you going to be able to replicate this recipe?" What a nice compliment.

Serve the ratatouille with parmesan and pine nuts as a vegetarian main dish. Or, as a side dish with a piece of grilled chicken. Or dice the chicken and add it to your bowl for a one-dish meal.

Servings: 5 to 6

Ingredients
>   2 tablespoons olive oil
>   ½ large red onion, diced
>   2 teaspoons coarse sea salt (or 1 teaspoon fine ground sea salt)
>   ¼ teaspoon cayenne pepper flakes
>   1 garlic clove, minced
>   4 large tomatoes, chopped (about 6 cups)
>   ½ cup chopped fresh herbs: basil, thyme, oregano, rosemary
>   (if you use dry herbs, cut amount in half)
>   1 bell pepper (any color), chopped
>   1 medium eggplant, chopped
>   1 medium zucchini, chopped
>   1 medium yellow summer squash, chopped
>   Grated parmesan cheese and pine nuts for serving

Directions
1. In a large pot over medium, heat olive oil.
2. Add onion, salt and cayenne and sauté until fragrant, about 5 minutes.
3. Add garlic and sauté for another minute or two.
4. Add tomatoes and herbs, cook until tomatoes are broken down, about 20 minutes.
5. Add pepper, eggplant, zucchini, yellow squash. Simmer until vegetables are slightly tender, about 20 minutes. Stir often.
6. Serve with parmesan and pine nuts.

Spring Rolls with Fried Tofu

This is a step and dish-intensive recipe, but it is well worth the effort. You can be creative and change up the vegetables, add a sauce, change the protein, etc.

Servings: 6 to 8 rolls

Ingredients

    8 ounces organic firm tofu
    ¼ teaspoon each: cayenne pepper, onion powder, garlic powder, sea salt
    ¼ cup flour (any type, I use cassava)
    Oil for frying tofu (I use coconut oil)
    8 small lettuce leaves
    4 chives, cut in half
    4 radishes, grated
    1 carrot, grated
    Thin rice noodles
    Rice paper
    Sesame seeds

Spring Rolls continued

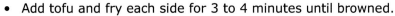

Directions

1. Prepare the tofu:
   - Cut tofu in ¼-inch slices and squeeze between a towel to remove excess water.
   - Mix the seasonings in with the flour.
   - Lightly dust tofu pieces in the flour/spice mix.
   - Lightly coat frying pan with oil, heat to medium-high.
   - Add tofu and fry each side for 3 to 4 minutes until browned.
   - Remove from pan, slice into ½-inch strips and set aside.

2. Cook rice noodles, drain, cut through several times and set aside.
3. Soften rice paper: in a large skillet, heat an inch or two of water almost to a simmer. Dip the individual rice paper in the warmed water for just a few seconds until soft.
4. Assemble the roll: on a flattened rice paper, add a piece of lettuce, a tofu slice, some carrots and radishes, ½ chive and some of the rice noodles. Sprinkle with sesame seeds. Turn the bottom and top of the rice paper in and roll the paper over the filling.

Spaghetti Squash Quinoa Fritters

If you have squash and swiss chard in the freezer from the harvest, these are a cinch to make. Even if you cook the squash and chard from scratch, they are still easy to make, just a bit more work to do all at once. These freeze well and are great to pull out for those meatless meals.

Servings: about 16 fritters

Ingredients

2 cups cooked spaghetti squash (see Harvest Staples)
2 cups cooked quinoa
1 cup chopped cooked Swiss chard
3 eggs, beaten
½ cup grated parmesan cheese
½ cup cornmeal
2 tablespoons chopped chives
2 garlic cloves, minced
Dash of cayenne pepper
Sea salt to taste
Olive oil for cooking

Directions

1. Hand mix all ingredients except olive oil.
2. Coat a skillet with olive oil and heat over medium-high heat.
3. Add ¼ cup mixture for each fritter to skillet, flatten out and shape.
4. Cook about 3 minutes on each side until golden and cooked through.
5. Add a small amount of oil to the skillet between batches to prevent it from becoming too dry.

Spaghetti Squash Quinoa Fritters continued

Important Notes

- To cook the Swiss chard, add ¼ cup water to a pan along with the chard and simmer until the chard is soft, about 7 to 8 minutes. You can chop the chard before or after cooking, but you want 1 cup cooked, chopped chard for the recipe.
- It's important to remove as much liquid as possible from the squash and chard, otherwise the cakes will be too soft. To remove the excess liquid from the squash and chard, place them in a colander and squeeze with a fork to drain off the liquid.
- The consistency of spaghetti squash can vary from squash to squash. If your batter is too watery, add more corn meal. If it is too dry, add another egg.

Summer Spaghetti

What a perfect meal for celebrating the garden bounty on a warm summer evening. I first had this dish at a friend's house in Italy and have been trying to recreate the YUM ever since. I only put measurements in the recipe to get you started. This dish just takes "some of this and some of that" so adjust according to what your taste buds tell you.

Servings: 4

Ingredients
  2 large ripe and juicy tomatoes, diced
  ¼ cup olive oil
  1 large clove garlic, minced
  ¼ cup chopped fresh parsley
  ¼ cup chopped fresh basil
  1 teaspoon sea salt
  ¼ teaspoon cayenne
  8 ounces spaghetti

Directions
  1. In a large serving bowl, combine all ingredients except spaghetti. Mix well, cover and let sit for 1 to 4 hours. This allows the flavors time to meld.
  2. When ready to eat, cook spaghetti. Liberally salt the water, as this adds to the flavor.
  3. When spaghetti is cooked, drain but do not rinse.
  4. Place the warm spaghetti in the bowl with the sauce, mix well and *mangia* (eat)!

Swiss Chard Cakes

These make a delicious meatless meal for lunch, dinner or even breakfast.

During the growing season when the chard is prolific and we can't keep up with eating it all, I blanch it for two minutes, immediately cool it off in an ice water bath, chop and freeze it. I freeze it in two-cup batches, which is just perfect for this recipe.

Servings: 6 to 8 cakes

Ingredients

¼ cup water (I use the water from cooking the Swiss chard or that comes out after defrosting it)
2 eggs, beaten
2 tablespoons olive oil, additional for cooking
½ teaspoon cumin
½ teaspoon sea salt
½ cup flour (I use sprouted garbanzo bean flour, but you can also use other flours)
2 cups chopped cooked and drained Swiss chard, stems included
1 small red onion, diced
2 chili peppers (Anaheims or poblanos), diced

Directions

1. In a large bowl, combine water, eggs, olive oil, cumin, salt and flour. Whisk until smooth.
2. Add Swiss chard, onion and peppers and mix.
3. Coat a large skillet with olive oil and heat over medium heat.
4. Drop ¼ cup batter into skillet, flatten and shape. Cook until brown on one side, flip and cook other side until browned and cooked through.
5. Serve with sour cream, butter, or nothing on top.

Tofu & Vegetable Fried Rice

This is a simple, flexible meal. Use whatever vegetables you have available. The key is to dice the vegetables so they are small and meld well with the rice. I often cut this recipe in half and make it as a one-meal skillet dinner.

Servings: 2

Ingredients

Coconut or olive oil
Seasonings to taste (turmeric, coriander, cumin is a tasty combination)
1 cup diced organic firm tofu, excess water removed
1½ cups diced vegetables
2 cups cooked black rice (or rice of choice)
Sesame seeds

Directions

1. Lightly coat the bottom of a skillet with oil and heat over medium heat.
2. Add seasonings and cook for 1 to 2 minutes until aromatic.
3. Add tofu and coat in oil and seasonings and cook for 2 to 3 minutes.
4. Add vegetables and cook until slightly tender, about 4 to 5 minutes.
5. Add rice to heat.
6. Sprinkle with sesame seeds and serve.

Veggie & Bean Tacos

When I make these, my husband puts the filling in a flour tortilla, smothers it in cheese and salsa and puts it under the broiler until the cheese is melted. I prefer the corn tortillas as shown.

Servings: 6 to 8 tacos

Ingredients
    1 tablespoon olive oil
    ¼ cup diced red onion
    2 garlic cloves, diced
    1 cup diced zucchini and yellow squash combo
    ½ red bell pepper, diced
    1 poblano pepper, roasted or fresh, diced
    2 cups (or 1 can) cooked beans (black, red or pinto)
    2 tablespoons diced fresh herbs
    Corn or flour tortillas
    Pumpkin seeds
    Cheese, shredded
    Salsa (see Side Dishes)
    Sea salt

Directions
1. In a skillet over medium, heat olive oil.
2. Add onions and sauté for a couple of minutes until tender.
3. Add garlic, squash and peppers and sauté until not quite tender.
4. Add beans and herbs, cook until heated through and flavors are melded.
5. Serve on warmed tortillas.
6. Sprinkle with pumpkin seeds, cheese, salsa and sea salt.

Zucchini Fritters

Yet another delicious way to use all that zucchini. Alongside a salad, these make a nice summer meal. I like to save the liquid I squeeze out of the zucchini and add it to soup or a smoothie.

Servings: about 18 fritters

Ingredients
    4 cups grated zucchini (see Directions, Step 1)
    2 cups cooked quinoa
    1 cup ground cornmeal
    1 cup crumbled feta cheese
    ½ cup diced red onion
    ¼ cup diced fresh oregano
    3 eggs, beaten
    1 teaspoon sea salt
    Olive oil for cooking

Directions
1. Grate the zucchini onto a clean dish towel, gather the four ends together, twist and squeeze as much liquid as you can out of the zucchini.
2. Mix all ingredients well.
3. To a large skillet, add enough olive oil to coat bottom and heat over medium-high heat.
4. Add ¼ cup of the mixture per fritter, flatten and shape with the back of a spoon.
5. Cook until browned and turn, about 2 minutes on each side.

🌿 Side Dishes 🌿

*Then he said to them, "Go your way, eat the fat and drink sweet
wine and send portions to him for whom nothing is prepared;
for this day is holy to our Lord; and do not be grieved,
for the joy of the Lord is your strength."* (Nehemiah 8:10)

I've always looked at side dishes as an afterthought until I realized
that I make them all the time. Sometimes I even plan my meal
around what side dish my taste buds are craving. Some of these can
double as appetizers as well.

Corn Muffins	120
Conversation Crackers	121
Easy Pickles	122
Jalapeños Cream Cheese	123
Red Cabbage	124
Roasted Vegetables	125
Salsa — 2 Ways	126
Spaghetti Squash —	
Southwest Style	127
Spanish Rice	128
Zucchini Hummus	129
Zucchini Parmesan Rounds	130

Corn Muffins

These muffins are a perfect complement to a salad, soup or a bowl of chili. They even go along nicely with scrambled eggs and vegetables. The only problem is that it's too easy to eat a lot of them.

Servings: 24 mini muffins

Ingredients
 ¾ cup cornmeal
 ¾ cup cassava flour
 ¼ cup tapioca starch
 2 teaspoons baking powder
 1 teaspoon sea salt
 1 cup milk of choice (dairy, almond, etc.)
 2 eggs, beaten
 3 tablespoons coconut oil, melted
 2 tablespoons maple syrup
 ½ cup corn kernels
 1 poblano pepper, diced

Directions
1. Heat oven to 375°F.
2. Grease 2 mini muffin tins (24 muffins).
3. Mix all dry ingredients together.
4. Mix all wet ingredients together.
5. Add wet ingredients to dry ingredients and mix well.
6. Mix in corn and pepper.
7. Fill muffin tins with the batter.
8. Bake for 20 minutes or until toothpick comes out dry.
9. Place on cooling rack to cool.

Variations
- Add ¼ cup diced herbs of choice.
- Make corn bread by baking in an 8 x 8-inch pan (increase baking time to 25 minutes).

Conversation Crackers

This recipe has nothing to do with gardening, or even with cooking for that matter. It does have to do with love though. It has such a nice story to go with it that I could not resist including it.

Pairing these cracker combinations with a bowl of soup makes for a nice meal.

Ingredients
    Your favorite crackers
    Your favorite topping

Directions
1. Liberally spread/place topping on crackers.
2. Enjoy.
3. Talk about the important things in life.

When my grandson Collin was between nine and 11, he spent a lot of time with me. When we needed a break, our favorite thing to do was sit at the table, spread butter on some crackers, crunch away and talk. One time I asked him, "So, Collin, what's your favorite thing about hanging out here?" His answer: "Everything." I'm still smiling.

Topping Options — use solo or stack (see photo)!
- Butter (that is our favorite)
- Jalapeno Cream Cheese*
- Zucchini Hummus*
- Pepperoni slices
- Plum tomato slice with diced jalapeno and feta
- Olives
- Sea salt
- Your favorite herbs
- Almond, peanut or sunflower seed butter

*See recipes in this chapter.

Easy Pickles

You might call this pickle deception, but I call it delicious! I gave a friend some fresh dill from the garden and to say thank you, she brought us a jar of pickles in which she used the dill. On the first bite of a pickle, my husband said, "Wow, this reminds me of the Fourth of July in my childhood." When we polished off the jar of pickles, my husband was about to throw the pickling juice down the sink and I said, "Wait, save that!" I cut up several pickling cucumbers from our garden, put them in the jar, put the jar in the refrigerator and voila: new pickles! Thank you, Patti, for the pickles.

Servings: 1 jar of pickles

Ingredients
1 jar of leftover pickling juice from your favorite pickles
Several pickling cucumbers

Directions
1. Slice cucumbers (peeling optional) in ¼-inch slices
2. Add to jar; be sure all slices are covered with the pickling juice.
3. Cover and refrigerate.
4. They are good to eat in about a week, but no need to wait that long if you don't want to.
5. That's it!

Jalapeño Cream Cheese

For those jalapeños that are just too hot to use otherwise, I find that if we finely dice them and add them to cream cheese, it negates some of the heat. This jalapeño cream cheese is delicious on bagels, sandwiches, crackers and celery.

Servings: 8 ounces of cream cheese

Ingredients
  1 eight-ounce tub of cream cheese
  2 jalapeños, finely diced
  1 tablespoon chives, diced (optional)

Directions
  In a medium bowl, mix all ingredients together. Return to tub for storage.

Red Cabbage

Each year I grow at least two red cabbages to make this dish, one for Thanksgiving dinner and one for Christmas dinner. I often grow a couple extra just in case I lose one or two to bugs or hail. This dish is easy to make, adds flavor and color to the meal and freezes well. It also makes the house smell amazing while it's cooking. When it's cooking, I like to go outside for a few minutes and then come back in the house just so I can get the full aroma!

Servings: 8 to 10

Ingredients

 1 head red cabbage, chopped
 2 tart green apples, diced
 ¼ cup red wine vinegar
 ¼ cup water
 ¼ cup brown sugar
 ¼ teaspoon ground cloves

This is a family recipe handed down through my father's side of the family. Each Thanksgiving and Christmas you could be sure this dish would adorn the table. It continues to be a family favorite, and now when we start talking about Thanksgiving and Christmas, my grandchildren say, "Grandma, are you going to serve that stuff with the red leaves?" Love in a cabbage.

Directions

 1. In a large pot, mix all ingredients together.
 2. Bring to a simmer, then turn heat to very low and cover.
 3. Cook for 1 hour or until desired tenderness.
 4. Stir often.

Roasted Vegetables

Roasted vegetables are an easy accompaniment to just about any meat dish. I serve them with meat loaf, BBQ beef or BBQ chicken sandwiches (see Main Dishes), grilled chicken and omelets. I will even use any leftovers chilled and mixed into a salad to bulk the salad up a bit.

The recipe below is for the ingredients shown in the photo. However, you can roast many different vegetables — sweet potatoes, rutabagas, butternut squash, zucchini, yellow squash, broccoli and more.

Servings: 3 to 4

Ingredients
> 2 turnips, peeled and chopped
> 2 purple potatoes, washed and chopped
> 2 red beets, peeled and chopped
> 2 golden beets, peeled and chopped
> 8 Brussels sprouts, washed and cut in half
> 2 tablespoons olive oil
> Sea salt to taste

Directions
1. Heat oven to 375°F.
2. Coat the chopped vegetables with the olive oil and sprinkle with sea salt.
3. Place vegetables on a roasting pan and spread so they are in a single layer.
4. Roast for 30 to 45 minutes, until desired tenderness or a bit longer for crispiness. Mix the vegetables every 15 minutes or so.

Note
> After you wash the vegetables, be sure to dry them in a towel. Otherwise the water will cause the vegetables to steam instead of roast.

Salsa — 2 Ways

Quick Garden Fresh Salsa
Here's how I quickly throw together a simple, fresh salsa to add to a meal. I only put quantities in to get you started; you'll quickly be able to make this your own version with quantities.

Servings: 1 to 2 cups

   2 cups chopped tomatoes
   ½ cup diced red onion
   1 poblano pepper, diced
   ¼ cup chopped cilantro or
   parsley (or both)
   Juice from half a lime
   Sea salt to taste

Combine all ingredients, mix well and serve.

Salsa with a Twist
At the end of the season one year, my husband was telling me a story about when he was single and used to make a salsa that he loved. I asked him if he had the recipe, which he produced after a bit of searching. We had just enough garden produce left to make a quart and enjoyed it over the next week. This is not a traditional Mexican salsa, but it is delicious just the same.

Servings: 1 quart

6 tomatoes, diced
1 large white onion, diced
4 Anaheim chili peppers, diced
1 jalapeño pepper, diced
1 clove garlic, minced (or ½ teaspoon garlic powder)
1 eight-ounce can black olives, diced
2 tablespoons olive oil
2 tablespoons apple cider vinegar
1 teaspoon sea salt

Combine all ingredients.

Spaghetti Squash — Southwest Style

This is a nice side dish to serve with chicken taquitos (see Main Dishes - Poultry) or grilled chicken. You can also make it a one-pot meal by adding diced, cooked chicken to it (see Southwest Spaghetti Squash in Main Dishes - Poultry).

Servings: 6 to 8

Ingredients
    2 tablespoons olive oil
    1 medium red onion, diced
    1 spaghetti squash, cooked and removed from shell (see Harvest Staples)
    2 cups (or 1 can) cooked black beans
    2 cups diced fresh tomatoes with juice
    1 cup corn kernels
    1 teaspoon cumin
    1 teaspoon paprika
    Sea salt to taste

Directions
    1. In a large saucepan over medium, heat olive oil.
    2. Add onion and sauté until just turning soft and fragrant.
    3. Add remaining ingredients. Mix well and cook until warm and flavors are melded, about 10 minutes.

Spanish Rice

Serve this with chicken fajitas or chicken taquitos (see Main Dishes - Poultry) and you have a perfect meal.

Servings: 4

Ingredients

> 1 tablespoon olive oil
> ½ medium red onion, diced
> 1½ cup short grain brown rice
> ¼ teaspoon cayenne pepper (more or less to taste)
> 1 teaspoon sea salt
> 1 cup tomato juice (from tomatoes, see below)*
> 2 cups water or chicken stock
> 1½ cups diced tomatoes, juice removed (for tomato juice above)*
> ½ cup corn kernels, fresh or frozen
> ½ cup peas, fresh or frozen

*Note: You need 3 cups of liquid. Use the liquid from the diced tomatoes and then add enough water/stock to equal the 3 cups. You can also use bottled/canned tomato juice for a portion of the liquid.

Directions

1. In a large pot over medium, heat olive oil.
2. Add onions and sauté until slightly tender, about 2 to 3 minutes.
3. Add brown rice, cayenne pepper and salt, stir to mix.
4. Add liquid and bring to a boil.
5. Turn to very low heat, cover and cook for 30 minutes.
6. Add tomatoes, corn and peas and cook covered for another 20 minutes.
7. Turn off heat and let sit for 10 to 15 minutes before serving.

Zucchini Hummus

This has become a seasonal favorite and is a great way to use up lots of zucchini. Even the grandchildren love it and it looks great on their faces!

This hummus dipped with homegrown cucumbers makes a perfect combination. It also tastes great on sandwiches, wraps, and with other vegetables, and freezes well.

Servings: 4 to 6 cups

Ingredients
6-8 cups chopped raw zucchini
¼ cup olive oil
¼ cup tahini
3 tablespoons lemon juice
1 cup sunflower seeds
3 cloves garlic
2 teaspoons paprika
1½ teaspoon sea salt
1 teaspoon cumin
1 teaspoon turmeric
¼ teaspoon cayenne pepper

Directions
Place all ingredients in a blender or food processor and blend until smooth.

Zucchini Parmesan Rounds

So simple, but OH so delicious. A great way to use the zucchini you didn't notice until it grew humongous. I must give credit to my nephew for passing along this recipe. Thank you, Kevin!

Servings: number of servings depends on how much you make

Ingredients
    1 large zucchini, sliced in ½-inch rounds
    Olive oil
    Grated parmesan cheese
    Dried or fresh oregano
    Sea salt

Directions
1. Heat oven to 350°F.
2. Lightly coat zucchini pieces with olive oil.
3. On a baking sheet, lay zucchini flat in a single layer.
4. Sprinkle each piece with parmesan cheese, oregano and sea salt.
5. Bake in oven for 15 minutes, then turn oven to broil and cook until cheese is browned, just a minute or two.

Variations
- Add some diced tomatoes.
- Add different herbs.
- Use eggplant slices instead of zucchini.

🍃 Desserts & Beverages 🍃

Pleasant words are like a honeycomb,
sweetness to the soul and health to the body.
(Proverbs 16:24)

The best part — healthy treats! When the grandchildren were young, I'd occasionally ask them if they would like a popsicle with their breakfast. It was fun to see their eyes open wide and they couldn't wait to tell their moms that grandma gave them dessert for breakfast. And then, of course, I had some explaining to do. All was well when I explained the ingredients!

Desserts

Applesauce — 2 Ways	132
Blueberry Cake	134
Chia Pudding	136
Fried Plantains	137
Fruit Crisp	138
Gummy Bears	139
Peach Gelatin	140
Plum Sauce	141
Popsicles — 4 Ways	142
Pumpkin Custard	145
Pumpkin Oatmeal Cookies	146
Pumpkin Pie	147
Rhubarb Apple Crumble	148
Rhubarb Bread	149
Rhubarb Raspberry Bars	150
Rhubarb Strawberry Compote	152
Rhubarb Strawberry Crumbles	153

Beverages

Herbal Root Beer	154
Smoothie — Basic	156
Smoothie — Pumpkin	157
Red Herbal Tea	159

Applesauce — 2 Ways

Each spring we talk about planting an apple tree, but we come to the same conclusion: why bother? The squirrels would eat all the apples. Our neighbors have an apple tree, and they finally gave up; it now serves as squirrel food all summer and fall (squirrels don't care if the apples are ripe). But there are a couple apples trees in the neighborhood from which I forage (with permission of course). Fresh, juicy, crisp and no wax. Nothing like it.

Applesauce — 2 Ways continued

Large Batch Applesauce
This applesauce freezes well; I freeze it in one and two-cup glass freezer containers.

Servings: 3 to 4 cups

> 12–15 apples
> Juice from half a lemon
> ½ cup water
> Optional: Add grated fresh ginger, cinnamon, pure maple syrup, raisins, chopped rhubarb.

Remove stems, core and pits and quarter apples (I leave the peels on). In a large saucepan, add apples, lemon, and water and mix. Cook over medium heat until desired consistency, about 20 to 30 minutes. Stir often. Crush the apples using a potato masher.
Enjoy chunky or blended.

Quick Applesauce
Here's how to make a single serving, quick applesauce. I often do this on cold winter days.

Servings: 1

> 1 apple

Wash, core and chop apple. Place in a small pan with 2 tablespoons of water and simmer covered until desired softness. Mash with a fork, add any desired toppings and enjoy. I eat mine right from the pan!

Blueberry Cake

I'm sure my childhood memories of this (see side bar) add so much to the flavor of this cake! This is my mom's recipe exactly as she made it. I substitute gluten free flour mix, coconut sugar, and non-dairy milk and it still tastes delicious. This is a thin cake; to make a thicker cake, bake it in a smaller pan (8 x 8-inch).

Servings: One 9 x 13-inch cake

Ingredients

Cake:
⅓ cup butter
¾ cup sugar
2 eggs, beaten
1½ cups flour
2 teaspoons baking powder
½ cup milk
1 teaspoon vanilla
2 cups fresh blueberries

Icing:
¼ stick butter
1½ cup confectioners sugar
3 tablespoons milk
1 cup fresh blueberries

Where I grew up on Long Island, N.Y., our home was surrounded by woods where all types of berries grew abundantly in the summer. My mom would often give me an empty coffee can and tell me to fill it up with blueberries. I knew those blueberries were going to turn into this cake, so I would run as fast as I could to fulfill her wish, my mouth watering the entire time (not to mention being full of blueberries as I popped some in my mouth!). We have a blackberry patch in our yard so our grandchildren can experience the fun of picking berries and popping them in their mouths. Love in a blueberry.

Blueberry Cake continued

Directions

Make the cake:
1. Heat oven to 375°F.
2. Grease a 9 x 13-inch baking dish.
3. Cream butter and sugar together.
4. Add eggs and cream into the mixture.
5. Mix and sift flour and baking powder.
6. Mix the milk and vanilla.
7. To the creamed mixture, add dry ingredients alternatively with the wet ingredients.
8. Add berries and fold in by hand.
9. Add batter to dish and bake for 20 to 25 minutes, until a toothpick comes out clean.

Make the icing:
1. Cream the butter, then add the sugar ¼ cup at a time while continuing to cream.
2. While adding the sugar, alternate adding the milk 1 tablespoon at a time; a little goes a long way. It should be a spreadable consistency, not too liquid and not too stiff.
3. Spread on cake to a uniform thickness and sprinkle with blueberries.

Chia Pudding

We had a variation of this for dessert at a local restaurant and enjoyed it so much that I decided to try to make it at home. It's now become a staple. It's delicious as a dessert, as breakfast, or an anytime snack, and there's no cooking involved! Pictured is the red, white and blue chia pudding I made one Fourth of July.

Servings: 4

Ingredients

1¼ cups milk of choice (dairy, almond, coconut)
⅓ cup chia seeds
2 tablespoons pure maple syrup
2 teaspoons vanilla
Chopped fresh fruit or fruit compote of choice
Toppings of choice (cacao nibs, coconut, fruit, berries, etc.)

Directions

1. In a bowl or 2-cup measuring cup, mix milk, chia seeds, maple syrup and vanilla. Stir well.
2. Cover and soak for 4 to 6 hours, or overnight, in the refrigerator and stir occasionally, if possible.
3. Mix pudding well to separate the seeds as much as possible.
4. Place a layer of fruit or compote in a single serving size container (I use 4 or 6-ounce jars).
5. Cover with the pudding.
6. Top with desired toppings.
7. Refrigerate until ready to serve.

Fried Plantains

No, I don't grow plantains, but they are still worthy to be included here. For years I shunned fried plantains because I couldn't imagine eating fried banana. One day on a whim, I picked one up from the store, fried it up and have been hooked ever since. The combination of the sweet from the plantain and salty from the sea salt melts in your mouth.

Servings: 2

Ingredients
1 plantain, very brown, peeled and sliced in ¼ to ½-inch slices.
Coconut oil
Sea salt

Directions
1. To peel the plantain, cut the top and bottom off and make a large cut with the tip of your knife down two sides of the plantain vertically. Pull the peel off as best you can, it can be a bit messy sometimes. Slice into ¼ to ½-inch slices.
2. Cover bottom of cast iron skillet (or other type of skillet) with coconut oil and heat over medium-high heat.
3. Fry plantain slices until brown on one side then turn over and cook the other side.
4. Remove and place on a paper towel.
5. Sprinkle generously with sea salt.
6. Eat while warm. Leftovers can be kept in the refrigerator and kept for a couple of days (that is, if you have leftovers).

Fruit Crisp

This recipe is great for a crowd and always delights. It serves 12+ and the recipe can easily be cut in half for a smaller dish.

Servings: 12

Ingredients

Filling options:

- 7 cups of peaches, peeled and sliced with one cup of blueberries or blackberries.
- 4 cups of chopped rhubarb and 4 cups of chopped strawberries mixed with 3 tablespoons real maple syrup or sugar and 1 teaspoon of vanilla.
- Or be creative. You need about 8 cups of fruit.

Topping:

½ cup melted coconut oil (more to grease baking dish)
3 cups rolled oats
1 cup chopped nuts (almonds, pecans, walnuts, macadamia nuts, any combination)
½ cup coconut sugar
½ cup real maple syrup
¼ teaspoon sea salt
2 teaspoons cinnamon

Directions

1. Heat oven to 350°F.
2. Grease a 9 x 13-inch baking dish with coconut oil.
3. Evenly spread filling into greased baking dish.
4. In a bowl, mix all topping ingredients.
5. Spread topping evenly over the filling.
6. Bake for 35 to 40 minutes until fruit is bubbling and topping is slightly browned.

Gummy Bears

These never fail to delight kids and adults alike. The recipe doubles very easily if you have a couple of molds to fill.

Servings: 34 gummy bears in pictured mold

Ingredients
¾ cup juice of choice
3 tablespoons gelatin
2 tablespoons honey

Directions
1. To a small saucepan, add juice, but do not turn on burner.
2. Sprinkle gelatin over top of juice, whisk to mix (the gelatin will not dissolve).
3. Let sit for 5 minutes.
4. Turn burner on low and heat juice until gelatin dissolves (be sure to keep heat low, as it will not take much heat to dissolve).

5. Whisk in honey.
6. Place gummy bear mold on a tray to give it stability.
7. Pour juice into mold and refrigerate until firm, about 2 hours.
8. Pop out of molds and enjoy!

Note
Although juice is plenty sweet, the gelatin tones down the sweetness and flavor. The honey provides some sweetness and flavor.

Peach Gelatin

Your mouth will burst with sunshine on the first bite of this treat. Each summer we buy several cases of peaches to enjoy some fresh and to freeze the rest for use throughout the winter. This is one of the most popular dishes we make from the peaches. You can freeze the required amounts of peach juice and cut up peaches (in separate containers) and then pull it out to make it for a fun, easy winter treat. Just add the gelatin and honey and assemble.

The first time I served this to my granddaughter Sonya (at seven years old), she had eight (small) helpings. Her five-year-old sister, Ashlyn, had six helpings. What an endorsement! Love in a peach.

Servings: 6

Ingredients
    4 peaches, pitted
    4⅓ cups water
    1 vitamin C capsule*
    2 tablespoons plain gelatin
    (same as used for the Gummy
    Bears)
    2 tablespoons honey

*The vitamin C capsule is optional. I open the capsule and pour the contents in the blender in Step 1 below to prevent the peaches from browning.

Directions
   1. To a blender, add 2 peaches, 4 cups of water and vitamin C and blend until smooth. Set peach juice aside.
   2. In a glass measuring cup, mix gelatin with ⅓ cup of water. Place measuring cup inside a small pot of hot water on stove and heat until the gelatin is dissolved.
   3. Add honey to gelatin and mix to dissolve.
   4. Mix gelatin mixture into peach juice.
   5. Pour into mold.
   6. Chop remaining 2 peaches and add to mold.
   7. Refrigerate until solidified.

Plum Sauce

This sauce is easy to make and a great way to use extra plums. This sauce tastes delicious by itself, on ice cream, pancakes, chicken, or just about anything you can imagine. Many recipes call for added sugar and spices, but I find I like it best with just the plums; the sweet and tart taste delights the imagination.

Ingredients
Plums
Optional: Cinnamon, orange juice, honey

Directions
1. Wash, pit and cut up the plums.
2. To a saucepan, add the plums with 2 tablespoons of water. Optionally, you can use orange juice in place of the water for an added layer of flavor.
3. Over low heat, cook until the plums are cooked down and the sauce is thick.
4. Add cinnamon and a taste of honey, if desired.
5. Blend to meld in the skins or run through a food mill to remove them.

Popsicles — 4 Ways

These are a delicious and healthy treat. You can also freeze these mixtures in gummy bear or other shaped molds for bite-size treats. Be forewarned: they can be habit-forming!

Servings: each recipe makes about 6 popsicles

Strawberry Rhubarb
    1 cup sliced rhubarb (½-inch pieces)
    1 cup full-fat coconut milk
    2 cups halved strawberries
    2 teaspoons vanilla
    1–2 tablespoons coconut sugar (optional)

In a saucepan, place the rhubarb and coconut milk and simmer until the rhubarb is very soft. Place mixture with remaining ingredients in a blender, blend until smooth. Pour into popsicle molds and freeze.

Peach
    3 cups of chopped fresh peaches
    1 cup full-fat coconut milk
    2 teaspoons vanilla
    1 tablespoon coconut sugar (optional)

Place all ingredients in blender and blend until smooth. Pour into popsicle molds and freeze.

Popsicles — continued

Orange Creamsicles

> 2 cups freshly squeezed orange juice, pulp included
> 1 can full-fat coconut milk
> 2 tablespoons honey
> 1½ teaspoons vanilla
> 2 drops food grade orange essential oil (optional)

In a saucepan, bring the orange juice to a boil, turn down to a low boil and cook until the liquid is reduced by half. Remove from heat and add remaining ingredients and mix. Pour into popsicle molds and freeze.

Root Beer Float

> 1 cup Herbal Root Beer syrup (see recipe in this chapter)
> 1 can full-fat coconut milk (you can also use water, which is the darker popsicle in the photo)
> 1 teaspoon vanilla

In a measuring cup, mix all ingredients. Pour into popsicle molds and freeze.

Pumpkin Custard

This is a delicious, easy way to enjoy pumpkin. It can be served warm or cold, with or without whipped cream.

Servings: 6 ramekins

Ingredients

Coconut oil
1 cup pumpkin purée (see Harvest Staples)
1 cup coconut milk
3 eggs, beaten
⅓ cup pure maple syrup
2 tablespoons molasses
1 teaspoon vanilla
1 tablespoon arrowroot
1 teaspoon cinnamon
¼ teaspoon ground ginger
¼ teaspoon sea salt

Here's an endorsement from grandson Joel (at nine years old): "Yummmm … Grandma, this is the most amazing thing I've ever tasted. Too much love! Grandma, you put too much love in it!" Love in a pumpkin.

Directions

1. Heat oven to 350°F.
2. Oil 6 ramekins with coconut oil and place ramekins in a 9 x 13-inch glass baking dish.
3. Mix wet ingredients in a bowl.
4. Mix dry ingredients in a small bowl.
5. Add dry ingredients to wet ingredients and mix well.
6. Pour mixture into ramekins.
7. To the glass baking dish, add warm water about half way up ramekins.
8. Carefully place baking dish in oven and bake for 50 minutes, until formed and a tooth pick comes out clean.
9. Remove baking dish from oven (carefully). Using tongs or a hot pad, remove ramekins from baking dish and place on wire rack to cool.

Pumpkin Oatmeal Cookies

It may be a funny looking smile on the cookie, but my grandchildren's smiles are beautiful when they know I've made these cookies just for them.

Servings: 24 cookies

Ingredients
- 1 cup pumpkin purée (see Harvest Staples)
- 4 tablespoons maple syrup
- 2 eggs, beaten
- 1 teaspoon vanilla
- 2 cups oat flour (grind about 2⅓ cups of oats in a blender)
- 4 tablespoons coconut sugar (or brown sugar)
- 2 teaspoons baking soda
- 1 teaspoon cinnamon
- 1 teaspoon pumpkin spice
- ¼ teaspoon sea salt
- 1 cup raisins

Directions
1. Mix all wet ingredients.
2. Mix all dry ingredients.
3. Combine the two and mix well.
4. Add raisins.
5. Cool in refrigerator for 30 minutes.
6. Heat oven to 350°F.
7. Place a very full tablespoon of batter per cookie on cookie sheet(s).
8. Bake for 10 minutes or until cooked through.

Variation
Substitute chocolate chips for the raisins. Or use ½ cup of each!

Pumpkin Pie

There are likely thousands of pumpkin pie recipes; this is how I make mine. Serve the pie by itself or topped with whipped cream, or even ice cream.

Servings: 1 pie

Ingredients

Pie crust of choice, unbaked
1½ cups pumpkin purée (see Harvest Staples)
⅓ cup pure maple syrup
2 tablespoons molasses
3 eggs, beaten
1 cup coconut milk
1½ teaspoon cinnamon
½ teaspoon nutmeg
¼ teaspoon cloves
¼ teaspoon allspice
¼ teaspoon sea salt

Directions

1. Heat oven to 425°F.
2. Mix pumpkin, syrup, molasses and eggs.
3. Add milk and spices and mix thoroughly.
4. Pour into pie crust.
5. Bake at 425°F for 15 minutes.
6. Turn oven down to 350°F and bake for 1 hour or until an inserted toothpick comes out clean.

Growing up, I never ate pumpkin pie and never paid much attention to it. It was not something that was served in our home. Then one year in my 40s, a friend invited me to Thanksgiving dinner and when I asked what I could bring, she said, "Pumpkin pie." Well, never mentioning that I'd never had it before, I set out to figure out how to make it. The result was delicious and I've enjoyed pumpkin pie ever since. But my real love affair with pumpkin began when I started growing pie pumpkins. As you've seen in this book, pumpkin is a staple in my diet.

Rhubarb Apple Crumble

This is a great dish for when summer meets fall — the rhubarb is finishing and the apples are fresh from the orchard (or from the foraging). Serve by itself, with vanilla ice cream, or whipped cream; either way, you won't be disappointed. You can also use frozen rhubarb, which means you can make this dish all through the winter.

Servings: 8

Ingredients

Filling:
3 large apples, cored and chopped
4 large rhubarb stalks, chopped
1 tablespoon coconut sugar
1 tablespoon lemon juice

Topping:
3 tablespoons nut meal (almonds, brazil, hazel, or a mixture)
3 tablespoons pecan pieces
3 tablespoons coconut shreds
2 tablespoons coconut sugar
2 tablespoons tiger nut flour (or other flour or increase nut meal)
1 tablespoon brown rice flour
1 tablespoon buckwheat four
2 tablespoons coconut oil
1 teaspoon vanilla
½ teaspoon cinnamon
Pinch of sea salt

Directions
1. Heat oven to 350°F.
2. Mix all filling ingredients and place in an 8 x 8-inch pan.
3. Mix all topping ingredients and sprinkle on top of fruit mixture.
4. Bake for 25 to 30 minutes, until bubbling and golden.

Rhubarb Bread

The combination of the sweeter ingredients with the sour rhubarb in this bread is very pleasing. It's a great way to use this delicious vegetable.

Servings: 1 loaf

Ingredients
- ½ cup cassava flour
- ½ cup coconut flour
- ½ teaspoon salt
- ½ teaspoon baking soda
- ½ teaspoon baking powder
- ½ cup coconut milk
- ½ cup applesauce
- 4 eggs, beaten
- ½ cup pure maple syrup
- ¼ cup coconut oil
- 1 tablespoon apple cider vinegar
- 1 teaspoon vanilla extract
- 1½ cups sliced rhubarb pieces (½-inch slices)

Directions
1. Heat oven to 350°F.
2. Line a bread pan with parchment paper and oil the ends where there is no paper. (This will help the bread come out of pan in one piece.)
3. Mix together the dry ingredients.
4. Mix together the wet ingredients.
5. Add the dry ingredients to the wet ingredients and mix well.
6. Add the rhubarb and mix well.
7. Pour in pan and bake for 1 hour or until toothpick comes out clean.

Variation
Make mini breads by dividing the batter into 4 mini-loaf pans. Bake for 30 to 35 minutes or until a toothpick comes out clean. These mini breads freeze well and make nice gifts.

Rhubarb Raspberry Bars

As much as I love the combination of rhubarb and strawberries, there comes a time each season when I get a bit tired of it and need a change. This is that change, and what a taste treat!

Servings: makes an 8 x 8-inch baking dish

Ingredients

Filling:
Note: this makes enough filling for 2 recipes. Freeze the other half or use as desired.
2½ cups sliced rhubarb (½-inch pieces)
1½ cups raspberries (frozen or fresh)
2 tablespoons of water or lemon juice
¼ cup coconut sugar (or sweetener of choice)
2 teaspoon tapioca starch

Crust:
1 cup oat flour (grind about 1¼ cup of oats in the blender)
½ cup oats
½ cup mixture of nuts or seeds of choice, ground
1 teaspoon baking powder
½ teaspoon sea salt
1 teaspoon cinnamon
½ cup brown sugar, lightly packed
½ cup melted butter or coconut oil

Rhubarb Raspberry Bars - continued

Directions

1. Make filling:
   a. In a saucepan, combine all filling ingredients except tapioca starch.
   b. Bring to a simmer and cook until fruit is softened, 10 to 15 minutes.
   c. Add starch, mix and cook for another minute until thickened. Turn off heat.
2. Make crust:
   a. Combine all dry ingredients except brown sugar and mix well.
   b. Add brown sugar. Mix well.
   c. Add butter or oil. Mix well.
3. Assemble and cook:
   a. Heat the oven to 350°F.
   b. Grease an 8 x 8-inch baking dish.
   c. Place half of the crust on the bottom of the dish and lightly pack it down so it covers the bottom and is even.
   d. Bake the crust for 15 minutes. Let cool.
   e. Spread half of the filling on top of the bottom crust.
   f. Lightly spread the remaining crust on top of the filling.
   g. Bake for 25 to 30 minutes until lightly browned on top.

Rhubarb Strawberry Compote

What a delicious way to eat rhubarb, not to mention straw-berries. Eat this compote by itself, put it on ice cream or cake, use it as a base for smoothies, or layer it with chia pudding. The recipe freezes well.

Servings: makes about 3 cups

Ingredients

2 cups chopped strawberries
2 cups sliced rhubarb (1-inch pieces)
¼ cup water
2 tablespoons sweetener (honey, maple syrup, cane sugar)

Directions

1. Place strawberries, rhubarb and water in a sauce pan and simmer until berries and rhubarb are broken down and soft.
2. Cool slightly and add sweetener.
3. Leave as is or purée to desired consistency.

Variation

Replace water with ½ cup of coconut milk.

Rhubarb Strawberry Crumbles

This is a nice, individual serving composition of a typical fruit crisp.

Servings: 6 ramekins

Ingredients

Crumble Topping:
1 cup tigernut or oat flour
(if using oat flour, you can
grind it in the blender from
about 1¼ cup of oats)
2 tablespoons arrowroot
starch
½ cup pecan pieces
3 tablespoons maple syrup
3 tablespoons coconut oil plus
more to grease the ramekins
1 teaspoon vanilla
¼ teaspoon sea salt

Filling:
2 cups strawberries, chopped
1½ cups sliced rhubarb (¼-inch pieces)
2 tablespoons coconut sugar
1 tablespoon arrow root powder

Directions
1. Heat oven to 350°F.
2. Grease ramekins with coconut oil and place in a 9 x 13-inch baking dish (this allows you to handle them as one unit).
3. Make crumble topping by combining all topping ingredients and mixing.
4. Make filling by combining all filling ingredients and mixing.
5. Place a small amount of topping in each ramekin, just enough to lightly cover the bottom.
6. Add filling to ramekins.
7. Top each ramekin with topping.
8. Place dish with ramekins in oven and bake for 45 to 50 minutes, until the top is browned and the filling is bubbling.

Herbal Root Beer

Now this is really *ROOT* beer! Made with a mix of herbal roots, it's what original root beer was: a healthy, refreshing, herbal tonic. Don't let that put you off; it tastes like, well, root beer! And it is! Even though nothing in the recipe is home grown (except the love) I had to include the recipe because it's such an essential part of my summer fun and it makes amazing root beer popsicles (see recipe in this chapter) and root beer floats.

You can buy the herbs at your local herb shop or at online herb stores. The syrup will keep in the refrigerator for about a month.

For Mother's Day one year, we invited our girls and their families over for a root beer float party and joke contest. We set up a serving bar for the floats, and as each person came through I gave them the choice of bottled root beer or homemade herbal root beer. My 13-year-old grandson Ethan said, "I want your root beer because everything you make is awesome!" Love in a root beer float.

This recipe was adapted from a recipe by Kimberly Gallagher of LearningHerbs.com (one of my favorite herb websites) by my sister Anne (an amazing gardener and cook), and is printed here with permission. I really can't take any credit for it other than making it and serving it and, not to mention, enjoying it.

Servings: makes about 2 cups of root beer syrup

Ingredients

    2 cups water
    1 tablespoon sassafras bark
    1 tablespoon astragalus root
    2 teaspoons sarsaparilla root
    2 teaspoons burdock root
    2 teaspoons dandelion root
    ½ teaspoon licorice root
    1½ cups dark brown sugar
    Chilled sparkling water for
    serving

Herbal Root Beer - continued

Directions
1. In a saucepan, add water and all roots.
2. Simmer covered for 30 minutes.
3. When cooled, strain liquid into a 3-cup or quart jar.
4. Add the brown sugar, mix well and chill.

To Serve
- Place 2 to 3 tablespoons of the syrup in an 8-ounce glass and add chilled sparkling water.
- Mix, taste, adjust by adding more syrup if desired.
- To make a root beer float, add vanilla ice cream.

Smoothie — Basic

I make this recipe during the warmer months of the year when fresh fruit, garden greens and herbs are bountiful. I don't add ice because I much prefer it at room temperature. You can add ice if you prefer yours cold. The ingredient list shows the base recipe, and from there I add in the listed options based on what I feel like having that morning.

Servings: 1

Ingredients

1 cup blueberries
1 small banana
1 handful greens, chopped (chard, kale, cilantro, spinach, etc. 1–2 cups)
3 tablespoons hemp seeds
1 cup liquid (water, herbal tea, vegetable broth, coconut water)

Directions

Add all ingredients to blender and process to desired consistency.

Add In Options

½-inch slice of ginger
1 teaspoon spirulina
Brazil nuts
1 tablespoon cacao nips (shown in the picture)
Yogurt
Kefir
Mint leaves

Smoothie — Pumpkin

This is a regular breakfast for me during the fall and winter months. It takes a minute to get the taste buds attuned since we are used to smoothies being cold, but on a cool fall or cold winter morning, this beats the cold anytime. I find a cold smoothie on a cold morning makes me cold all day; using the hot water in this warms me up.

Servings: 1

Ingredients
½–¾ cup pumpkin purée (see Harvest Staples)
1 banana
¼ cup pecans (walnuts or almonds are good too)
2 tablespoons flax or hemp seeds
1 tablespoon tahini
1 teaspoon pumpkin pie spice (or just cinnamon)
1 handful of greens (dandelion, spinach, chard, parsley, or kale)
1 tablespoon pure maple syrup
Pinch of sea salt
½-inch slices of ginger and turmeric (optional)
1 teaspoon powdered rose hips (optional)
1 cup hot water

Directions
1. Place all items in a blender and blend until smooth.
2. Add more liquid to desired consistency if necessary.

Variation
Use heated herbal tea or chicken stock as the liquid base in place of the water.

Red Herbal Tea

This is a refreshing summer tea. I buy the loose teas in bulk at our local herb shop (you can also find them online) and keep a jar of each on hand. It's my go-to beverage to serve when company comes over. I chill it in the refrigerator and serve it either cold or over ice. If the weather is cooler, I'll serve it at room temperature or hot — it tastes great at any temperature. You can sweeten it but I find it's not necessary, as the flavor is so rich and smooth. Garnish it with mint or lemon balm if you have either growing.

Servings: makes 1 quart

Ingredients
    2 teaspoons hibiscus tea
    2 teaspoons rose hips
    2 teaspoons rooibos tea

Directions
    1. Combine ingredients in a tea strainer.
    2. Place the strainer in the mouth of a quart jar.
    3. Pour boiled water through the tea strainer to fill the jar.
    4. Steep for 30 minutes.
    5. Remove tea strainer and chill in the refrigerator.

Note
    Tea bags are also readily available for each of the teas in this recipe. If you prefer to use teabags, use two of each to replace the loose teas.

Yes, you are seeing things correctly – that's a zucchini dressed in a cowgirl outfit! One year our neighbors left a huge zucchini on our doorstep. We decided to go shopping for "zucchini clothes" and dressed it up and left it back on their door step. The next day, a ransom note appeared on our door: *$10,000 or the zucchini gets shredded.* Needless to say, the zucchini appeared back on our door step the next day, shredded. Don't you wish you had such fun, crazy neighbors!

 Index

A

Apples
Applesauce – 2 Ways 132
Rhubarb Apple Crumble 148

B

BBQ
BBQ Beef Sandwiches 64
BBQ Chicken Sandwiches 78
BBQ Sauce 6

Beef
BBQ Beef Sandwiches 64
Beef & Okra Stew 65
Beef Stew 67
Beef Stew – Nightshade Free 68
Beef & Vegetable Skillet 66
Bratwurst in a Zucchini 69
Meatloaf 70
Shepherd's Pie 71
Spaghetti Squash with
    Meat Sauce 72
Spaghetti Squash Taco Pie 73
Taco Meat on Potatoes 74
Unstuffed Cabbage 75

Beets
Beet Salad 44
Roasted Vegetables 125
Root Veggie Shred 54

Beverages
See Table of Contents for
    Desserts & Beverages 131

Black Beans
Black Bean Soup 22
Black Bean Skillet 99
Black Bean Tostadas 100
Veggie & Bean Tacos 117

Blueberries
Blueberry Cake 134
Chia Pudding 136
Fruit Crisp 138

Butternut Squash
Butternut Squash Soup 24
Southwest Stew 91
Roasted Vegetables 125

C

Cabbage
Chopped Salad 48
Coleslaw 49
Mixed Cabbage Blue Cheese
    Salad 52
Red Cabbage 124
Red Cabbage Salad 53
Unstuffed Cabbage 75

Carrots
Carrot Salad 46
Coleslaw 49
Root Veggie Shred 54

Cauliflower
Cauliflower Soup 25

Chicken
BBQ Chicken Sandwiches 78
Chicken Cakes 79
Chicken & Cauliflower Pasta 80
Chicken Fajitas 81
Chicken Fried Rice 82
Chicken Pesto Salad 47
Chicken Skillet 83
Chicken Soup 26
Chicken Stock 27
Chicken Taquitos 84
Chicken Tomatillo Soup 28
Millet Skillet 86
Pasta with Pesto & Chicken 87
Pesto Pizza with Chicken 88

INDEX

Quinoa with Chicken &
    Vegetables 89
Southwest Chicken Soup 35
Southwest Spaghetti Squash 90
Southwest Stew 91
Spring Pasta 93
White Bean & Vegetable Soup 40

Corn
Corn Muffins 120
Corn Salad 50

Cucumbers
Chopped Salad 48
Cucumber Salad 51
Easy Pickles 122
Tomato & Cucumber Salad 56

D

Desserts
See Table of Contents for
    Desserts & Beverages 131

E

Eggs
Eggs Poblano 101
Frittata 102
Ramen Soup 33

Enchilada Sauce
Enchilada Sauce 9
Spaghetti Squash Taco Pie 73
Taco Meat on Potatoes 74

F

Fritters
Spaghetti Squash Quinoa
    Fritters 112
Zucchini Fritters 118

G

Gelatin
Gummy Bears 139
Peach Gelatin 140

Green Beans
Green Beans, Freezing 10
Green Bean Vegetable Soup 29

K

Kale
Beef & Vegetable Skillet 66
Chicken Skillet 83
Mung Dal & Basmati Rice 104
Quinoa with Beans & Vegetables 108
Shepherd's Pie 71
Smoothie – Basic 156
Smoothie – Pumpkin 157
White Bean & Vegetable Soup 40

M

Millet
Millet Skillet 86

O

Okra
Beef & Okra Stew 65

P

Pasta
Chicken & Cauliflower Pasta 80
Pasta with Pesto & Chicken 87
Spring Pasta 93
Summer Spaghetti 114

Peaches
Fruit Crisp 138
Peach Gelatin 140
Popsicles – 4 Ways 142

Peppers
Cayenne Pepper 7
Jalapeño Cream Cheese 123
Pickled Jalapeños 12
Poblano Peppers, Roasted 13

Pesto
Chicken Pesto Salad 47
Pasta with Pesto & Chicken 87

Pesto Pizza with Chicken 88
Pesto 11
Pizza with Tofu 106
Turkey Sandwich – 5 Ways 94

Pizza
Pesto Pizza with Chicken 88
Pizza with Tofu 106

Popsicles
Orange Creamsicle 143
Peach 142
Root Beer 143
Strawberry Rhubarb 142

Potato
Potato Soup 31
Taco Meat on Potatoes 74
Shepherd's Pie 71

Pumpkin
Pumpkin Cream of Buckwheat 107
Pumpkin Custard 145
Pumpkin Oatmeal Cookies 146
Pumpkin Pie 147
Pumpkin Puree 14
Pumpkin Smoothie 157
Pumpkin Soup 32

Q

Quinoa
Quinoa with Beans &
   Vegetables 108
Quinoa with Chicken &
   Vegetables 89
Spaghetti Squash Quinoa
   Fritters 112
Zucchini Fritters 118

R

Rhubarb
Fruit Crisp 138
Popsicles – 4 Ways 142
Pumpkin Cream of Buckwheat 107
Rhubarb Apple Crumble 148
Rhubarb Bread 149

Rhubarb Raspberry Bars 150
Rhubarb Strawberry Compote 152
Rhubarb Strawberry Crumbles 153

Rice
Chicken Fried Rice 82
Mung Dal & Basmati Rice 104
Spanish Rice 128
Tofu & Vegetable Fried Rice 116

Root Beer
Popsicles – 4 Ways 142
Herbal Root Beer 154

S

Salad
See Table of Contents for Salads
   & Dressings 43

Sauces
BBQ Sauce 6
Chimichurri Sauce 8
Enchilada Sauce 9
Pesto 11
Tomatillo Sauce 18
Tomato Paste 19
Tomato Sauce 20

Smoothies
Basic 156
Pumpkin 157

Soup & Stock
See Table of Contents for Soup 21

Spaghetti Squash
Roasting Spaghetti Squash 15
Spaghetti Squash with Meat
   Sauce 72
Spaghetti Squash Taco Pie 73
Southwest Spaghetti Squash 90
Spaghetti Squash Quinoa
   Fritters 112
Southwest Spaghetti Squash 127

INDEX

Stew
Beef & Okra Stew 65
Beef Stew 67
Beef Stew – Nightshade Free 68
Southwest Stew 91

Swiss Chard
Chicken Skillet 83
Green Bean Vegetable Soup 29
Mung Dal & Basmati Rice 104
Sausage Vegetable Noodle Soup 34
Shepherd's Pie 71
Spaghetti Squash Quinoa
    Fritters 112
Steamed Vegetable Soup 36
Swiss Chard Cakes 115
White Bean & Vegetable Soup 40

T

Tofu
Avocado Toast with Fried Tofu 98
Miso Soup 30
Millet Skillet 86
Pizza with Tofu 106
Spring Rolls with Fried Tofu 110
Tofu and Vegetable Fried Rice 116

Tomato
Caprese 45
French Dressing 60
Ratatouille 109
Salsa – 2 Ways 126
Spaghetti Squash with Meat
    Sauce 72
Tomato & Cucumber Salad 56
Tomato Paste 19
Tomato Sauce 20
Tomato Soup 37
Unstuffed Cabbage 75

Tomatillos
Chicken Fajitas 81
Tomatillo Sauce 18

Turnips
Red Cabbage Salad 53
Turnip Sausage Skillet 96

Vegetarian
See Table of Contents for
    Main Dishes – Vegetarian 97

Z

Zucchini
Bratwurst in a Zucchini 69
Zucchini Fritters 118
Zucchini Hummus 129
Zucchini Parmesan Rounds 130
Zucchini Salad 57
Zucchini Soup 41

🌿 About the Author 🌿

O taste and see that the Lord is good!
Blessed is the man who takes refuge in him!
(Psalms 34:8)

What fun it has been compiling and writing this cookbook. It's taken several years and was prompted because each year I had to figure out how to make things all over again. I decided to document my recipes and this cookbook was born. I have no culinary training other than the school of life and watching my mother cook amazing food for our family. My father would come in from the garden with his arms loaded with vegetables and say to my mom, "Dear, do your magic." And before you know it, the family was sitting down to something delicious and nutritious.

In my early 20s, I went to college to study agriculture. My dream was to have an organic farm — that was in the mid 1970s. That dream never faded, but life took me in other directions. Next I studied nutrition, then languages, then business. Along the way I finally graduated, but in the meantime I worked on building a career. The first 15 years of my career I spent in international sales, the next 20 years in technical and business writing. One of the great joys of my life was providing a foster home to three middle school aged girls (not all at the same time!). Then how blessed I was to meet and marry a wonderful man later in life, who brought along with him my beautiful step daughter. My husband built me my first garden in 2008. It brought me back full circle to my love of organic gardening. Life has been full and God has blessed me with so much; I cannot help but be thankful in all things.

To contact the author, email
linda@greenthingscooking.com